Grappling
with the
Good

SUNY series, The Philosophy of Education

Philip L. Smith, editor

Grappling with the Good

Talking about Religion and
Morality in Public Schools

Robert Kunzman

State University of New York Press

Published by
State University of New York Press, Albany

© 2006 State University of New York

For information, address State University of New York Press,
194 Washington Avenue, Suite 305, Albany, NY 12210-2384

Production by Michael Haggett
Marketing by Susan M. Petrie

Library of Congress Cataloging-in-Publication Data

Kunzman, Robert, 1968–
  Grappling with the good : talking about religion and morality in public schools /
Robert Kunzman.
    p. cm. — (SUNY series, the philosophy of education)
  Includes bibliographical references and index.
  ISBN 0-7914-6685-X (hardcover : alk. paper)
  ISBN 0-7914-6686-8 (pbk. : alk. paper)
1. Religion in the public schools—United States. 2. Moral education—United States.
I. Title. II. SUNY series in philosophy of education.

LC111.K86 2006
370.11'4—dc22

                                                                                                2005014015

ISBN-13: 978-0-7914-6685-8 (hardcover : alk. paper)
ISBN-13: 978-0-7914-6686-5 (pbk. : alk. paper)

                    10 9 8 7 6 5 4 3 2 1

Dedicated to the memory of

Jenny B. Farnham

grandmother
and
public school teacher

1915–1979

Contents

Foreword

Americans have become accustomed to hearing that public education is in a state of crisis. Unfortunately, agreement about the nature of the crisis is in short supply. On the left of the political spectrum, chronic under-funding for schools, especially the schools of the urban poor, is the prime grievance, with the failures of desegregation coming in a distant second. On the right, public education is condemned for its insulation from the discipline of the market and its alleged hostility to Christian values. If we cannot even agree on the nature of the problem, no one should be surprised that real dialogue on solutions is rare.

Rob Kunzman's superb book also addresses a crisis in American education, though the crisis he identifies cuts across the stale polarities of current educational debate. The crisis Kunzman discerns has to do with a failure of mutual understanding and respect in a nation that is increasingly pluralistic and where the dialogue necessary to secure understanding and respect is an urgent but largely unrecognized educational task. Like educational critics on the left, Kunzman argues for an education that embodies ideals of equality at the core of America's democratic tradition. Like critics on the right, he acknowledges that merely by evading deep ethical diversity public education cannot respect the divergent creeds and traditions that students bring to the public school.

Kunzman's interpretation of pluralism carries him far into questions at the cutting edge of contemporary political philosophy. These are questions about how we can find a basis for morally stable social cooperation when so many of our differences prove to have no rational resolution. He rejects the tempting route that so many take who claim that once we neatly sunder religion from ethics we can find terms of cooperation easily enough. Kunzman is acutely sensitive to the depth of religious faith in citizens' lives and to the pervasive ways in which it conditions our ethical perceptions and beliefs. A public education which accepts that truth must find new ways of educating students for citizenship in a pluralistic society. Perhaps the principal merit of Kunzman's book is that he describes such ways through rich examples of classroom dialogue that would acknowledge our pluralism without compromising the necessity of common educational ends. This is one of those very rare books from which both teachers and scholars would profit.

EAMONN CALLAN
STANFORD UNIVERSITY

Acknowledgments

What I have to say in this book has emerged in part from my ongoing experiences teaching in public schools, nowhere more importantly than Champlain Valley Union High School in Vermont. I will always be indebted to my friends and colleagues there. Even now, the best part of my day is often the time I spend teaching in the local high school, and for that opportunity I remain indebted to Rachel Nichols, a gifted teacher and generous classroom partner. Many thanks as well to my colleagues in the Indiana University School of Education for their support of my writing and teaching about these issues in the university context, but also for encouraging my ongoing teaching in the K–12 setting.

Many people have read versions of this book over the past several years, providing valuable insight and suggestions. These friends and colleagues have included Morva McDonald, Ira Lit, Jon Levisohn, and Marlissa Hughes. Rob Reich deserves special thanks for his helpful guidance and support at multiple stages of the writing process. Sam Intrator, a brilliant writer and teacher who understands the classroom as well as anyone I know, spent many hours helping me organize, reframe, and clarify. I also enjoyed many conversations about these issues with my late colleague and friend Kipchoge Kirkland. I will miss Choge's warm encouragement and deep insight; he had so much more to say and teach us.

I am also grateful for the numerous mentors who have nurtured my thinking and writing over the years. Larry Cuban, Denis Phillips, David Tyack, and Lee Yearley have all lent their wisdom and encouragement to my endeavors; they are teachers in the best sense of the word. I must also single out Eamonn Callan, who gave the great gift of helping me become a better thinker. His unfailing support and keen analytical mind have helped shape this book, even while he graciously disagrees with some of what I have to say.

I have no doubt that with everyone mentioned, had I listened better to their suggestions, I would have here a stronger book. I hope they will excuse me for the times I somehow ignored their good advice. I also appreciate the opportunity to share my emerging thinking in various publications; portions of this book have appeared in earlier forms in the *Journal of Philosophy of Education, Journal of Moral Education, Religious Education, Theory and Research in Social Education, Philosophy of Education 2003*, and *Philosophy of Education 2005*.

While this book has benefited greatly from the advice of many reviewers, I have also relied on other people who don't know much about it beyond the general topic. They support my work, but more importantly, they support me. Gene and Lucy Kunzman, my first and best teachers, have given steady love and encouragement since literally day one. Bill and Katy White remain devoted friends who care for my family beyond human measure. I have read many acknowledgements in which the author apologizes to his children for the ways in which his scholarly efforts have shortchanged their time together. Hannah and Kira, my hope is that you have not felt this too often, and that you have gained something from watching your father work hard on a project about which he cares deeply. Regardless, your smiles always put academia in perspective. Finally, the person taking care of those girls—even in the midst of her own career—deserves my greatest gratitude. Audra, your patience and support have made this project possible; your love has made our walk together rich with joy.

Central to democratic thought as I understand it is the idea of a body of citizens who reason with one another about the ethical issues that divide them, especially when deliberating on the justice or decency of political arrangements. It follows that one thing a democratic people had better have in common is a form of ethical discourse, a way of exchanging reasons about ethical and political topics. The democratic practice of giving and asking for ethical reasons, I argue, is where the life of democracy principally resides. Democracy isn't all talk. Now and then there is also a lot of marching involved, for example. But there is no form of ethical life that generates more talk on the part of more people than does modern democracy. It is in democratic discourse that the claims and reasons of marching protestors get expressed. Protestors rarely just march. They also carry signs that say something. They chant slogans that mean something. They sing songs that convey a message. And they march to or from a place where speeches are given.

—Jeffrey Stout, *Democracy and Tradition*

1

Introduction

It was early in my high school teaching career, in the middle of a discussion about human cloning. Cheryl had been arguing for limits on scientific research, and her hand shot up again from the back of the classroom. "We shouldn't play God," she insisted.

Maybe not, but can we talk about God? Or at least about the ways in which religious beliefs influence our lives together in a diverse society? Cheryl made her comment in the midst of an eleventh-grade English class discussion of Aldous Huxley's *Brave New World*. The chilling images of the Hatchery, where embryos on conveyor belts were genetically modified, had struck a chord with my students.

Truth be told, I wasn't really sure where to go with Cheryl's assertion. I knew that her religious faith played a major role in her life, and she was responding to some classmates who were advocating nearly unbridled genetic manipulation in the pursuit of disease-free, physiologically superior humans. Asking Cheryl a follow-up question would likely spark a vast array of student opinions about religious belief and its role in society and public policy. Should I really open *that* can of worms?

I should have, but I didn't. Instead, I maneuvered around the comment and sought to refocus attention on the story: "OK, some people do see religious belief as important in discussing an issue like gene manipulation—but what's the larger point Huxley might be trying to make here about society and technology and the pursuit of perfection?"

It seemed to me at the time that if we pursued Cheryl's comment, the likelihood of arriving at some sort of respectful conclusion to the controversy was pretty remote. In my defense, any experienced teacher could probably add a few more reasons to steer clear of the issue. If an administrator had been observing my class, she probably would have complimented my deft handling of a potentially volatile topic.[1]

But it didn't feel like a fine pedagogical moment. Instead, my evasion left me with some profound questions: How do we help students engage thoughtfully with ethical disagreement, even when religion is involved? And how do we make decisions about how to live together respectfully—in spite of our disagreement—in this diverse society? This book argues that we can and should help students learn how to talk about religion and morality, learn how to discuss disagreements that are influenced by religious and other ethical perspectives—not because we can "solve" them, but because this grappling is the responsibility of informed, respectful citizenship.

A DEFINITION OF "ETHICAL EDUCATION": MORE THAN MORALS

While the subtitle of this book mentions "talking about religion and morality," some greater precision is necessary as we move forward. Throughout this book, I will use the key term *ethical education* to represent a much broader realm than is usually meant by the more familiar labels of moral, civic, or character education. This is a crucial distinction with particularly significant implications for the role of religion. Bernard Williams reminds us that—unlike our modern conception—the ancient notion of ethics included not only a focus on moral obligation, but also a concern for what makes a full and meaningful life.[2] Ultimately, ethics are concerned with the question, "How should one live?" So whereas much

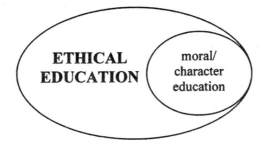

modern civic and character education is concerned primarily with our responsibilities toward others, ethical education also involves broader questions about the good life and human flourishing.

Why is it important to focus on the broader question of "the good life" instead of just on "right and wrong"? The simple answer (which I will explain more fully in chapter 3) is that for many people, determinations of what is right and wrong are made in light of their understanding of what makes a full and meaningful life. This is often the case when religious belief is involved—Cheryl's strong resistance to genetic manipulation, for example, emerged from her ethical conception of God as a creator whose designs should not be altered.

Ethical education seeks to explore questions as wide-ranging yet potentially interrelated as:

- What kind of life should I lead? What kind of person should I try to become?
- How can I live a full and meaningful life?
- What and whom can I trust?
- How can I tell right from wrong? What are my obligations toward others?
- Do my obligations vary according to the nature of my relationships with others?
- How do I deal with suffering, my own and that of people around me?
- How do I weigh my needs and desires against those of the larger community?
- How should I respond to disagreement about issues of vital importance to me?
- When am I justified in criticizing others? When are they justified in criticizing me?
- Does human life have transcendent meaning?

Even within moral psychology, a field long dominated by narrower Kohlbergian notions of justice and obligation, some are calling for greater attention to these broader ethical concerns. Lawrence Walker, for example, criticizes the overemphasis on moral rationality and obligations toward others. "Morality is also an intrapersonal exercise," he points out, "because it is integral to the how-shall-we-then-live existential question—it involves basic values, lifestyle, and identity." Because of this link between moral obligation and broader ethical concerns, it is oftentimes misguided to discuss questions of right and wrong without also discussing beliefs about human flourishing, what some psychologists are now calling one's broader "moral identity."[3]

One way in which this link manifests in our lives together as citizens is the degree to which many Americans draw on their religious convictions when taking positions on public policy: same-sex marriage, genetic engineering, private school vouchers, the Pledge of Allegiance, and abortion are just a few prominent examples. The growing religious diversity of Americans only adds to the array of ethical perspectives represented. As a result, our public discourse is infused with ethical arguments based on religious beliefs, often with competing visions of "the good life." This has powerful implications for a model of citizenship that includes participation in such discourse—it requires citizens who can thoughtfully and respectfully "grapple with the good" as it is envisioned by a range of religious and other ethical perspectives. If we believe that public schools play a vital role in fostering thoughtful citizenship, then it seems vital that they help students learn how to talk about these ethical differences.

The students in my English class missed out on this important element of citizenship, and they aren't alone. A few years ago, students across the nation studied civics while wearing bracelets adorned with the letters WWJD—"What Would Jesus Do?" But it's quite likely neither they nor their non-Christian classmates ever discussed how deeply held religious beliefs should most appropriately relate to laws and policies that affect all citizens. "If someone believes life begins at conception, how should this influence her position on stem cell research?" "Should my tax dollars support schools based on ethical beliefs I reject?" "Can we compromise on public policies when competing religious views are at stake?" The bracelets have mostly disappeared, but the challenge of religiously-informed citizenship remains largely ignored in our public schools.

Why is an ethical education that grapples with these tough issues, and helps students learn to talk together respectfully about them, so important? Some may recall what happened in the summer of 2002, when the University of North Carolina assigned students, for summer reading, a book called *Approaching the Qur'an*, an annotated set of excerpts from the Koran. What followed were lawsuits in federal court, legislative threats to cut the university budget, and comments that compared it to the teaching of Hitler's *Mein Kampf*. Many students criticized the assignment as well. One remarked, "I don't really care about [Muslims] right now. I'm not in an enlightened state of mind. If anything, I want to worry about ourselves, and turn to our own religion."[4] What strikes me most powerfully about this incident is the unwillingness or inability of many observers and students to engage thoughtfully with ethical diversity, in this case to explore questions such as "What is it in Islam that makes 1.2 billion people, many of them our fellow citizens, see it as meaningful—and how does it influence their views about our life together?" I believe the health of our increasingly diverse society depends on people who can communicate and deliberate respectfully among differing and often unfamiliar ethical perspectives.

This book contends that schools' continued avoidance of ethical controversy bodes ill for our civic capacity for informed and respectful discourse. My argument strives for a middle ground of sorts, acknowledging the importance of being able to understand and engage with the religious convictions of fellow citizens, while also guarding against the dogmatic imposition of religiously informed policies that affect all of us. I strive to identify the civic and educational principles that underlie this tension, and offer a vision for how educators can help prepare students to engage thoughtfully and productively with ethical conflict in our public square.

While these pages will include some philosophical arguments to support my claims and educational recommendations, it should be clear from our national and local conflicts that "grappling with the good" is very much a part of our everyday lives. Certainly the events of September 11, 2001, have raised a multitude of issues about religious and ethical diversity and how we navigate this diversity both at home and abroad. In addition, questions surrounding the idea of separation of church and state seem particularly salient now. The courts appear to be nearing a crossroads regarding how we conceive of this relationship. Whereas past decades have seen legal emphasis on avoiding governmental entanglement with religion, now the "free exercise" portion of the disestablishment clause is receiving growing attention; religious citizens, the argument goes, should have the freedom to see their convictions reflected in the public arena.

In spite of this ongoing tension in the public square and its obvious implications for our lives together, versions of my English class "pedagogical evasion" episode play out in classrooms throughout the country, and extend across the curriculum. I want to emphasize, however—the avoidance is broader than just the role of religion. While sometimes the potential presence of religion motivates teachers to steer clear, the prospect of grappling with *any* substantive ethical issue can be enough to change the subject. Summarizing her own research and that of others, Katherine Simon observes, "Although moral and existential issues arise frequently, they are most often shut down immediately. If moral issues are not shut down completely, they are often relegated to assignments for individuals, rather than explored in public classroom discussion."[5] Whether the controversy focuses on stem cell research, gender roles, or our responsibility to others in our community, teachers and schools frequently avoid or downplay the ethical issues involved, particularly when they are informed by religious perspectives. The educational result, I contend, is a citizenry with little skill in discussing ethical controversies, particularly as they relate to religion, and thus even less sense of how to make decisions about living together in respectful and reasonable disagreement.

Ironically enough, our public schools certainly don't suffer from a lack of curricular resources when it comes to "moral education" or "character education" as it is currently conceived. As researcher James Leming noted back in 1995, "It is almost impossible to find a school district that doesn't have some sort of moral education program," whether it be focused on an issue such as drug use or conflict resolution or a broader effort such as character education. Since that time, attention to and funding for such programs have only increased.[6]

But as I will argue, something deeply important is missing from most of these conceptual and curricular approaches, both in terms of depth and breadth. The current focus on acontextual, prescriptive virtues typical of much character education curricula lacks the complexity inherent in most ethical challenges we face. Even those approaches that push students to wrestle with greater complexity do not generally provide sufficient opportunity for them to engage with the deeper ethical sources (religious and otherwise) that often inform our lives outside the classroom.

THE FOCUS OF THIS BOOK

This book describes and justifies a partial approach to ethical education that I call *Ethical Dialogue*. I use this label as a shorthand throughout the book, but it does not signify a formal program or technique. Ethical Dialogue involves cultivating empathic understanding of unfamiliar ethical perspectives and then engaging in thoughtful, civic deliberation in light of this understanding. While such a process should be tailored to the developmental level of students, I contend that Ethical Dialogue is an approach to ethical education appropriate and important for all grade levels.

As I have explained, ethical education should help students explore questions about the good life and human flourishing, and understand the different ways people answer those questions. Many such ethical issues are not only woven into the way we live our lives but are features of school life as well. Even if not directly explored through intentional classroom curricula, they are addressed in the very texture of the school community. Relationships between and among students and staff, modeling of attitudes and beliefs by adults and peers—the entire social fabric abounds with ethical commentary. In many school settings (especially larger, more impersonal milieus), the responses can be bewildering and even incoherent, but students learn from them nonetheless. A full consideration of ethical education—and even my narrower focus of Ethical Dialogue—needs to take this broader social landscape into account. For reasons of scope and depth, my goal with this book is less ambitious, limited to the formal classroom curriculum as an (important but insufficient) element of ethical education.

Obviously, this limited focus has its drawbacks. Extensive research has demonstrated the importance of community in schools and classrooms in fostering prosocial outcomes. The broader "social web" plays a vital role in promoting or discouraging students' ethical growth.[7] A teacher who plans curricular experiences for her students cannot ignore these wider social conditions—inside of school and out—in which students live. In fact, it is the dissonance between the messages of the broader society and much ethical curricula that often renders them ineffectual and even hypocritical. The school environment itself can overwhelm the best ethical education taking place behind a particular classroom's door. When anonymity and self-advancement are the overriding features of broader school life, a single classroom that nurtures mutual understanding and respect for others will find its influence sadly muted.

The "hidden curriculum" messages that students receive are not all negative, however, and opportunities for ethical education extend well beyond schools themselves. Families, communities, and civil society play influential roles in helping students consider the relationship between their own ethical perspectives and broader society. In particular, extensive research has been conducted on the value of service activities in encouraging ethical growth, through exposure to the processes and structures of civic engagement and the opportunity for youth to incorporate civic involvement into their own developing identities.[8]

Clearly, this broader realm of ethical education is far too complex to address completely in this book. While I certainly do not claim that my argument for Ethical Dialogue in public school classrooms represents a wholly sufficient approach to ethical education, I believe a focused consideration of such a process can play an important role in helping our students talk and live together respectfully across ethical difference, and thus contribute significantly to their ethical growth and the health of civic society.

My book is also limited in its focus on public schools. This is not to say that Ethical Dialogue is not possible in private schools, secular or religious. In fact, I see public schools—for legal reasons as well as the challenges of ethical heterogeneity among constituents—as perhaps the most challenging setting for Ethical Dialogue (excluding, of course, strongly sectarian private schools that have no interest in thoughtful engagement with ethical difference). If my argument for Ethical Dialogue proves compelling and plausible in the public school context, then I believe it would prove even more so in a private school setting that shared similar commitments to mutual understanding and deliberation.

This is obviously not the first book to advocate improved ethical understanding in schools, nor is it the first to argue that students should develop a commitment to respectful deliberation and the skills necessary for it. But it is less common for the former approach to address how deeper mutual understanding can contribute to civic deliberation; likewise, arguments for deliberative democracy—rarely focused on K–12 schools in the first place—generally devote less attention to the process of developing *substantive* appreciation of the ethical frameworks that inform our deliberation. This project insists on a strong connection between the two: civic deliberation is a vital skill in an ethically diverse society, but a deliberative outcome without a substantial groundwork of mutual understanding lacks moral justification.

THE STRUCTURE OF THIS BOOK

My approach involves an interplay of sorts between theory and practice. Chapter 2 describes the historical and legal terrain of ethical education, arguing that U.S. public schools have moved from a reliance on a single dominant ethical source (pan-Protestantism) to an almost complete avoidance of ethical sources altogether. This avoidance has been manifested in the past four decades in the curricular models of values clarification, cognitive developmentalism, and character education.

In chapter 3 I offer a philosophical argument for why this avoidance of deep ethical sources often fails to demonstrate respect and ultimately hinders our capacity to engage in just civic deliberation. In situations of ethical conflict, respect requires understanding the ethical frameworks of those with whom we disagree. This chapter also sketches the contemporary American religious landscape and seeks to explain some of the dissonance between current ethical education and the religious-ethical frameworks of many students.

Chapter 4 describes the vital process of "imaginative engagement," wherein students strive for empathic understanding of unfamiliar ethical perspectives. More than mere propositional knowledge, imaginative engagement combines both "head and heart" and is a crucial precursor to the process of civic deliberation addressed in chapters 5 and 6. This chapter also discusses some pedagogical strategies that seek to foster imaginative engagement.

Since the attempt by people to fulfill their differing visions of the good life will frequently result in conflict, decisions will need to be made about how we will live together; this process of civic deliberation is the focus of the next two chapters. In chapter 5 I draw crucial distinctions between the private, civic, and political realms and describe the qualities of "deliberative reason" that we should be helping students develop. Chapter 6 considers more closely the role of religion in civic deliberation.

Chapter 7 explores the implications of a commitment to Ethical Dialogue for teacher education. Teachers need to develop a basic understanding of the topics being discussed and gain skill in facilitating thoughtful, respectful discussion. In addition, schools need to nurture in teachers a *commitment* to Ethical Dialogue, a recognition of its vital importance for both students' education and the health of civic society. In light of these demands, I endorse a conception of teacher education that extends well beyond the initial year or two of preservice experience and that emphasizes the importance of peer collaboration in preparing teachers for Ethical Dialogue.

A LEARNING PROCESS

It has been sixteen years since I began teaching in public schools, and in this time I've thought a great deal about these issues, both from the perspective of a classroom practitioner and an educational theorist. Even now as a university professor, I still teach an eleventh-grade English class in the local public high school, and so am regularly reminded that the challenges of fostering Ethical Dialogue are substantial. There are days when, if you visited my high school class, you would question whether I am qualified to prepare future teachers or write these books. Certainly the adolescents I teach have raised such questions! Simply put, good teaching is very hard work, and Ethical Dialogue adds to the challenge. Anyone familiar with K–12 schools and classrooms will find the prospect of Ethical Dialogue demanding and even daunting. My intent here is not to present Ethical Dialogue as a quick or easy formula, but as something worth our aspiration and ongoing commitment.

In spite of my arguments here, I realize that plenty of teachers will find good reason to avoid such risks in their classrooms, as I did a dozen years ago with Cheryl and *Brave New World*. But the alternative—an inability to engage thoughtfully and respectfully amidst increasing social and ethical diversity—is even more perilous. As David Purpel rightly contends, "No set of issues is as explosive, controversial, emotional, and threatening as moral and religious disputes. None is more vital."[9]

2

Evading the Ethical

How We Got Here

The opening pages of this book described one of my own public school teaching experiences when ethical issues arose during discussion, and my hesitation and uncertainty in how to proceed. If I *had* followed the ethical thread, we could have explored a variety of perspectives about genetic engineering and even considered what different and differing beliefs (religious and otherwise) informed those perspectives.

But if you will permit the blatant scientific anachronism, consider how this discussion of cloning from the early 1990s would have played out differently in classrooms of the 1790s, 1890s, or even 1950s. As this chapter will explain, ethical education in U.S. public schools prior to the mid-twentieth century rested almost entirely on pan-Protestantism as its informing ethical source. So there would likely have been little hesitation in appealing to the Protestant Bible as authoritative and definitive. Any consideration of how some people might view genetic research differently if they were atheists or Buddhists, for example, would almost certainly be absent. Whatever was deemed sinful or prohibited by Protestant theological doctrine would be presented as ethical truth, and acceptance of this truth would be assumed to be a duty and manifestation of responsible American citizenship. The notion of dialogue with differing ethical perspectives would likely not have occurred to most schools or communities.

In the last half century, the terrain of ethical education has changed for public schools, but certainly not in a way that has provided curricular or pedagogical clarity. For most schools and classrooms, the shift has been away from ethical conversation altogether. When "right" and "wrong" are discussed, participants rarely have the opportunity to consider the deep ethical sources (religious or otherwise) that inform those convictions. When they do, controversy often follows. Simply put, American society is deeply ambivalent about the role of religion in public schools. This chapter seeks to explain how we got here, from a landscape of ethical monism to evasion and ambivalence.

TRACING THE PATH TO AMBIVALENCE

A system of government that makes itself felt as pervasively as ours could hardly be expected never to cross paths with the church. In fact, our State and Federal Governments impose certain burdens upon, and impart certain benefits to, virtually all our activities, and religious activity is not an exception. The Court has enforced a scrupulous neutrality by the State, as among religions, and also as between religions and other activities, but a hermetic separation of the two is an impossibility it has never required.[1]

So observed the U.S. Supreme Court in 1976, and the distinction between neutrality and separation remains a constant negotiation in our national life, nowhere more powerfully and importantly than in our schools. What also seems clear is our continued ambivalence about the role of ethics and religion in public schools. Consider a few examples that have appeared in newspapers over the past several years:

- When Vancouver, Washington, area high schools made a 2002 field trip to a "youth summit" to hear the Dalai Lama speak about compassion and nonviolence, several state legislators formally protested the event as being religious in nature and thus improper. In particular, they complained that a double standard existed whereby non-Christian religious perspectives were given far greater leeway for expression in public schools.[2]
- A federal district court partially upheld a 1999 parental lawsuit against the Bedford Central School District (NY), which charged that the school promoted religion through an Earth Day ceremony, constructing the likeness of a Hindu god, and the sale of "worry dolls." The latter two claims were eventually dismissed on technicalities, and ultimately a federal appeals court deemed the Earth Day ceremony legally acceptable. A spokesman for the People for the American Way Foundation, who defended the district, characterized the suit as "yet another attempt by

the right-wing folks to use legal challenges to substantially interfere with school district curriculum."[3]

- A federal judge in Detroit ruled in 2004 that the Ann Arbor school district was responsible for a Roman Catholic student's legal fees after unjustly censoring her views on homosexuality during a "Diversity Week" program organized by the school's Gay-Straight Alliance. Elizabeth Hansen sought to express her religiously-informed perspective that she was unable to "accept religious and sexual ideas or actions that are wrong," but the school insisted that this and references to shifting sexual orientations be excised from her speech.[4]

- And finally, when first-grader Zachary Hood and his classmates were invited to bring their favorite books to school, he brought his *Beginner's Bible*. His teacher, however, refused to let him read his selection entitled "A Big Family," which recounted Jacob's reunion with his brother Esau. Zachary's mother filed suit, and a series of courts ruled in favor of the school's decision. Columnist George Will remarked, "Reread 'A Big Family,' substituting the names, say Kevin and Bruce for Jacob and Esau. If *that* makes a constitutional difference, courts have built a wall of separation between the Constitution and common sense."[5]

A regular scan of almost any newspaper, in fact, will reveal ongoing disputes over the role of religion in public schools and in particular their approaches to ethical education. Such ambivalence and disagreement are not only expressed in the legal system, of course. Evidence suggests that the bulk of citizen complaints to local school boards involves religious issues as well. These controversies are not likely to subside, either, given our increasing ethical diversity. "At the dawn of the new millennium," historian James Fraser observes, "the peoples of the United States are more secular, especially in their public culture, more religious, in many different private forms, and more diverse than ever before in the nation's history."[6]

How did this relationship between ethics, religion, and the public schools develop through our national history? To tell the comprehensive story of ethical education in U.S. history would take a full book by itself, if not a series of volumes. A narrowing of focus, then, seems an important first step. This chapter is not intended as a full depiction of religious diversity in American educational history; minimal scholarship regarding minority religious practice renders such a summary impossible, even if space permitted here. Rather, I offer a sketch of how Protestant domination of emerging American values and culture has affected public school policy and practice, particularly in the realm of ethical education.[7]

The historical and legal aspects of the relationship between religion and public schools can be separated roughly into four basic groups: governmental financial support for schools, government oversight and regulation of schools, religious activity and observance in schools, and religion within the academic curricula. Since my focus in this book is on the level of classroom practice, I give primary attention to historical elements involving school curricula. Nevertheless, each of the four groupings has contributed to the shifting relationship between religion and public education and thus merits some attention.

My goal in this chapter is to describe the relationships between ethics, religion, and public schools in America as an unfolding process over the past three centuries. I argue that while ethical education in public schools began rooted in a singular ethical source (various religious denominations whose values were merged into a pan-Protestantism), this connection gradually weakened until the 1960s, when schools began to address ethical education in abstraction from deep ethical sources, religious and otherwise—an approach that largely continues today.

Some readers may object to this characterization of our current situation, pointing to the ongoing, periodically successful attempts to bring religious (usually Christian) doctrine into the public schools through issues such as creationism, sex education, Bible groups, and prayer. These efforts vary by region and are perhaps significantly underreported. What seems important to recognize about these manifestations of "school as cultural battleground," however, is their general purpose of capturing political and curricular ground, rather than fostering dialogue and student learning across diverse ethical perspectives. In this sense, such efforts seek a return to ethical education rooted in a single ethical source rather than helping students understand and navigate the diversity of ethical sources that influence our lives together as citizens.

With this tension in mind, I conclude the chapter by proposing an approach to ethical education that reframes the judiciary's recent philosophical shift from separation to neutrality. Public school curricula must be more than an inert collection of ethical diversity; students need to learn how to engage respectfully with ethical difference. While we should certainly not return to our educational origins wherein a singular ethical source dominated, neither can we separate our moral and civic responsibilities to explore ethical disagreement from the very sources that inform that diversity. Understanding the still-unfolding relationship between ethics, religion, and public schools may help us appreciate the challenge and potential of ethical education moving forward.

COLONIAL ORIGINS AND ETHICAL ASSUMPTIONS

Believing with you that religion is a matter which lies solely between man and his God, that he owes account to none other for his faith or his worship, that the legislative powers of government reach actions only, and not opinions, I contemplate with sovereign reverence that act of the whole American people which declared that their legislature should "make no law respecting an establishment of religion, or prohibiting the free exercise thereof," thus building a wall of separation between church and state.[8]

This conviction of Thomas Jefferson, expressed during a presidential letter to the Danbury Baptist Association in 1802, has served as a cornerstone legal image of the appropriate role of religion in American society, and nowhere more than public education.

While this metaphor has become a familiar one, our understanding of the nature of this wall has shifted drastically since Jefferson's letter. As many advocates of school prayer are fond of pointing out, this metaphor is not to be located in any founding American documents and did not actually appear in judicial decisions until the mid-twentieth century. Prior to the 1850s, the idea of separation between church and state was more popularly one of *distinction* rather than *separation*, and was concerned more with the disestablishment notion of keeping government out of religion rather than vice versa. It wasn't until the common school disputes between Protestants and Catholics (which I address in the next section) that the idea of keeping religion out of government became a central concern in American life.

Education in the American colonies varied by region, but nowhere did anything resembling a system of schools exist. While Thomas Jefferson, Noah Webster, and Benjamin Rush began to urge the formation and support of more standardized public schools following the Revolutionary War, Americans were content to leave education—and especially ethical education—in the hands of families and communities.[9] Nonetheless, the issues of ethics and specifically religion in state-sponsored education trace their origins to the colonial period. In order to understand the educational system that ultimately emerged, we need to recognize the intertwined relationship between church and state as it developed from these origins.

Whatever religious motivations early colonists had, they focused on freedom to practice their particular faith rather than on cultivating an atmosphere of religious pluralism. Virginia, followed later by the Maryland, Georgia, and Carolina colonies, established the Church of England as the required and subsidized state religion. Similarly, Puritan Congregationalism became the established faith in the colonies of Massachusetts, Connecticut, and New Hampshire. Those who wished to depart from the official faith were forced to strike out on their own. Roger Williams presaged the move toward separation of civil and religious authority with his Rhode Island settlement. Pennsylvania and Delaware had a similar lack of religious establishment. Other colonies, such as New York, New Jersey, Maryland, and Georgia, experienced changing religious establishments as religious populations within their borders changed. Still others, at varying pre-Revolution times, experimented with systems of multiple establishments in attempts to support diversity of belief. New York, for instance, required each town to underwrite a church and minister, with majority vote determining which (Protestant) denomination would be financed.[10]

The European settlers may have brought with them their ideas of each being the one true church, and even endeavored to establish political states in line with those beliefs, but this faded as the Revolution brought new political realities into play. While the Senate would not endorse Madison's proposed restrictions on states' rights in supporting religious education, much public financing of religion had already begun to recede, and with the advent of the Constitution and the Bill of Rights, only four states after 1791 continued to use public funds for religious support. Most newly admitted states avoided state religion establishment laws altogether.[11]

Nevertheless, even while establishment began to fade, religion, ethics, and education remained firmly intertwined. From 1690 until the first part of the nineteenth century, the most common schoolbook in the colonies was the *New England Primer*, which focused on the nature of God and believers' relation to God. The McGuffey Readers, introduced in 1836, dominated the latter part of the century; they also sought to teach ethical lessons but did so with a steadily decreasing number of direct references to God. This shift, coupled with the emergence of the common school movement, represented a profound transformation in the history of American education. Warren Nord claims that between the American Revolution and the dawn of the twentieth century, "religion dropped by the wayside as America marched into the modern world." This description is too extreme, as later sections in this chapter will attest; nevertheless, churches had already surrendered their control over public education, and the previously inextricable link between ethics and religion in American education was beginning to loosen.[12]

COMMON SCHOOLS IN SEARCH OF COMMON ETHICS

The common school movement of the mid-nineteenth century emerged from a political conviction that the growing diversity of the American population—with all the ethical and civic concerns such a phenomenon raised in some citizens—required a strong acculturative mechanism. Of particular concern to educators and politicians alike were the growing number of Catholic immigrants, especially in urban areas. This emphasis on a unity of experience stemmed in part from the lessons of the past. As Carl Kaestle notes, "European history did not augur well for the survival of republics, and developments in America suggested the dangers of cultural diversity and regional loyalties." With the continuing waves of immigration, seemingly endless frontiers, and national ideals of individualism, statesmen and educators alike felt the need for a unifying ethos. In New York City, for instance, the foreign-born population increased from 11 percent of the total population in 1825 to over 50 percent just thirty years later; half of these immigrants were Irish Catholic. This influx continued through the end of the nineteenth century as well, with the U.S. Catholic population expanding from 6 million in 1880 to 14 million by 1910. As Charles Glenn observes, "*E pluribus unum* was not an idly chosen motto."[13]

Another impetus for the development of common schools, argues B. Edward McClellan, was in response to the denominational rivalries fostered by the Second Great Awakening earlier in the century. The common school notion of nonsectarian moral training provided a setting and opportunity for social cohesion while sidestepping doctrinal disagreements. But this cohesion—at least initially—was achieved only among Protestants. The intended unifier turned out to be a forced Protestant Christianity, which ultimately distorted both the faith and the principles of unity it was intended to promote. Common school reformers and Protestant supporters too often directly equated one with the other, as in the words of one prominent advocate: "The principles of democracy are identical with the principles of Christianity."[14]

The most famous of the common school reformers, Horace Mann championed the establishment of common schools in the Northeast. His emphasis on vague nonsectarianism earned him the enmity of both Catholics (who saw a clear pan-Protestant bias in his vision) and orthodox Protestants (who initially despised what they viewed as watered-down religion). Mann's idea of salvation was the pursuit of ideas as exemplified in the life of Jesus, not necessarily faith in him as savior. At least equal to Mann's concern about Papism was his worry that the economic gap between rich and poor and the political controversies of the day would generate a social chasm that would ultimately destroy the nation. Fierce battles were being waged, for instance, over slavery, immigration, and women's rights, and Mann urged schools to seek ideological shelter in the "common" values of local communities.[15]

William H. Ruffner, a Presbyterian minister who became state superintendent of Virginia schools in 1870, argued for a similar blend of moral training and common religion. Called the "Horace Mann of the South," he also had to contend with critics who pushed for more or less religious influence in schools. African American churches also played a pivotal role in the development of public schooling, which began largely from the efforts of newly freed slaves following the Civil War. In many cases, churches—black and white—served as the first school buildings in the postbellum South, and the separation of secular and religious instruction was virtually nonexistent.[16]

Part of the common school reformers' target was private schools. By 1840, the distinctions between public and private schools existed largely as we now understand them, and reformers believed that the acculturative effects of common schools would be lost if too many children attended private schools outside the reach of the assimilative, morally focused, patriotic, state-sponsored education. In line with his desire to lessen the class divide, Mann urged professionals to enroll their own children in common schools, at least at the elementary levels.[17]

In addition to political motives, some common school advocates shared a postmillennial vision of bringing about God's kingdom on earth and the final victory of Christian principles in both law and culture. This was particularly true of the Midwest and Northwest regions. Common school reform began to take shape in the Midwest by the 1850s, led by evangelical ministers determined to build and sustain a Protestant nation. These efforts faced greater resistance in rural areas, where the increased taxes—necessary for improved facilities, longer school terms, and the addition of secondary programs—were often rejected by voters.[18]

A similar missionary zeal existed in the Northwest. The dual purposes of moral and civic commonality carried the day here as well, David Tyack observes, with minister-educators "determined to prevent Americans from using their mobility and their open spaces to flee from responsibility. If neglected, the frontiersmen would not only be prey to Satan's wiles but also a threat to the republic." The school and the church served as mutual reinforcers of the postmillennial vision, although one important distinction stood out between them. While ministers fought over the church attendance of every last settler, a truce existed in the realm of public education, likely in response to the threat of Catholic schools, which in the minds of some Protestant clergy were worse than no schools at all. Much as in the East, a pan-Protestant common school emerged. The Portland Public Schools superintendent's words in 1882 echoed his brethren in the East: "The American public school has been built up, and is still upheld, by the great mass of sensible Christian people who believe in a vital connection between religion and morality . . . this body of our people does not intend to support a school emasculated of all the sacred sanctions of morality and delivered over into the hands of the apostles of the new secular philosophy."[19]

Common school reformers shared an assured belief in the mutual underpinnings of their educational faith. Many scholars argue, however, that common school advocates such as Mann did not see themselves as promoting their personal religious beliefs. Rather, they operated under the popular assumption that the ethical training deemed essential in staving off social fragmentation required a general religious foundation. "Nearly everyone found a purely secular public education simply inconceivable," Stephen Macedo claims, and "many people viewed Protestantism as inseparable from the American republican idea."[20]

Much speculation has arisen regarding the underlying motives of common school reformers, but my focus in this chapter is on effect more than motivation, and in this respect the record seems clearer. Many Catholics, for instance, bitterly opposed the common schools' pan-Protestant agenda and argued against public taxation for common schools, claiming the state was establishing an educational, religiously biased monopoly. This led to the ironic result—in light of reformers' critique of private schools—of generating an increasing determination by Catholics to expand their parochial school system. By mid-century, Catholicism was the single largest religious denomination, and this—coupled with a papal encyclical calling for worldwide Catholic education—caused Catholic schools to multiply and flourish.[21]

No argument between Catholics and the common schools was more explosive than that of Bible reading. Tyack and others explain the chain of reasoning behind nineteenth-century common schools and Bible reading:

> [Protestants] assumed a congruence of purpose between the common school and the Protestant churches. They had trouble conceiving of moral education not grounded in religion. The argument ran thus: To survive, the republic must be composed of moral citizens. Morality is rooted in religion. Religion in based on the Bible. The public school is the chief instrument for forming moral citizens. Therefore, pupils must read the Bible in school.

But Catholics objected to the almost exclusive use of the King James Bible in classrooms. The practice of reading the Bible without comment was the centerpiece of nonsectarian moral education, since all Protestant denominations were in favor it. Even if greater flexibility had existed over Bible versions, this didn't solve the problem for Catholics. While Protestants viewed the Scripture as a wholly sufficient guide for Christian living, Catholic interpretations of the Bible were strictly guided by additional church teachings. Emotions ran so high in 1844 as to result in the Philadelphia Bible riots, which killed thirteen and left a Catholic church in ashes.[22]

While Mann's vision of common schooling arguably did not involve use of the Bible as a devotional tool, many teachers and administrators apparently saw its classroom value as including far more than civic purposes. For example, an 1869 resolution of the National Teachers' Association (forerunner to the National Education Association) stated that the Bible should be "devotionally read," and a late nineteenth century NEA conference presentation urged continued proclamation of "needed religious truth and sanctions into all our schools," admonishing teachers to not only teach about Christianity but also appeal to such doctrine in enforcing proper student behavior.[23]

But to what extent *was* the Bible actually read in common schools, and was conflict the regular outcome? Benjamin Justice argues that Bible reading was far from a universal practice in common schools, and that the highly publicized urban conflicts over religion in schools did not reflect the "peaceable adjustments" that local communities often made in response to such disputes. While Justice's argument provides a helpful correction to perceptions of constant educational turmoil, the validity of his assertion applied nationally remains uncertain at best, for at least three reasons. First, Justice focuses specifically on New York State history; it is quite conceivable that other regions of the country—such as the South, with its more fluid boundaries between school and church—encouraged significantly more Bible reading. Second, an absence of local conflict does not necessarily indicate a peaceful environment in which various constituencies felt heard and respected; even today, for example, many non-Christian minorities quietly endure the Christmas "season" in schools rather than suffer the wrath of a local community that feels its cultural traditions are being spoiled. Finally, it seems the historian may have to settle for a certain degree of agnosticism about actual religious practices in schools. Teachers often avoided publicizing the presence of religion in their classrooms in order to avoid controversy. Even today, most teachers will acknowledge that what they do behind their classroom doors is rarely observed or documented; but if the NTA and NEA excerpts cited earlier are any indication, many teachers in that era saw their role as moral educator in religious terms.[24]

While the nature and emphasis of Protestant-based moral education almost certainly varied according to locality, common schools did serve as battlegrounds for citizens seeking to include, impose, or preserve their own ethical frameworks in the civic realm. Reformers such as Mann recognized that the colonial models of ethical education directed by singular ethical sources (highly sectarian Protestant frameworks) would not nurture or sustain a broader civic commitment in a diverse society. Their advocacy of a more widely acceptable religious framework met with resistance, however, both from orthodox Protestants who decried the diluted ethical vision and from those who perceived such "nonsectarianism" as still very Protestant biased indeed. The essential question of how to foster an effective and just civic realm amidst growing ethical diversity remained; as the century turned, signs of a gradual shift away from religious sources for ethical education began to emerge.

THE GRADUAL SHIFT TOWARD CIVIL RELIGION

The first U.S. Supreme Court ruling on Bible reading didn't occur until 1963, but twenty-one states heard cases prior to that, and most ruled the practice constitutional. In the first such case, fifteen-year-old Bridget Donahoe was expelled from her Maine public school for refusing to read the Protestant version of the Bible, and she took her case to court in 1854.

Her legal claim was based on an argument against the tyranny of majority rule, in this case (and across the country) of Protestantism. The court, however, sided with the school, discounting the religious argument by maintaining that the Bible was used as a reading text, not for purposes of religious instruction.[25]

Two decades later, however, in *The Board of Education v. Minor*, the Ohio Supreme Court reversed a lower court decision and ruled that religious education was unconstitutional in Ohio public schools. The court charged Bible reading advocates with equating religion with Christianity, effectively designating Christianity as the religion of the state. Judge Welch advocated a "hands-off" doctrine: "Let the state not only keep its own hands off, but let it also see to it that religious sects keep their hands off each other." This case also made the significant articulation that pan-Protestantism was unjustifiably exclusionary, an idea still contrary to the popular assumption of the time.[26]

The degree to which religion was being pushed out of public education at the close of the century is a disputed matter, however. Warren Nord, echoing Samuel Windsor Brown's 1912 argument in *The Secularization of America*, contends that "textbooks, the official curriculum, and the governing purposes of education had become almost completely secular by the end of the nineteenth century. Indeed, the fact that a ceremonial religious shell continued to envelop public education into the twentieth century only helped obscure the fact that its substance was now almost entirely secular." Other scholars criticize these depictions of dominant secularization in schools in the late 1800s, arguing that religion was not in retreat but simply subordinated to other ends, its presence still very much alive. The *Minor* case in Ohio and an 1890 case in Wisconsin—both dealing with Bible reading—were not indicative of the range of decisions; the general inclination of courts was to support opt-out policies for dissenters rather than outlaw religious elements in the curriculum. The Wisconsin case decision even included the claim that religious beliefs held by all faiths would not be sectarian in nature and thus could be taught. Justice William Penn Lyon listed two such beliefs: "the existence of a Supreme Being, of infinite wisdom, power and goodness, and that it is the highest duty of all men to adore, obey, and love Him. . . . Concerning the fundamental principles of moral ethics, the religious sects do not disagree." The assumption of a common religious core to guide ethical life still persisted.[27]

While it seems fair to say that the religious grounding of much ethical education remained, these connections did start to become far less explicit in the early twentieth century. The first three decades—amidst perceived threats to social stability such as World War I, the Bolshevik Revolution, and the Roaring Twenties—saw a call for stronger moral standards and prompted the development of "character education." The Character Education Association, for example, was founded in 1911 and promoted "ten laws of right living." Similarly, the NEA sought to develop a common core of religious instruction—focused on the existence of God and high ethical standards—that would be acceptable to Protestants, Catholics, and Jews. Such "common" precepts were quite similar to the principles generally cited by contemporary character education curricula, and both movements suffer from similar shortcomings addressed later in this chapter.[28]

The growing progressive movement was fairly critical of such character education, believing that lists of virtues were unhelpful in a complex and morally relative world. Its approach to ethical education was even less connected with religious frameworks, focusing instead on the child's experience as the source of ethical growth. In April 1930, the annual convention of the Progressive Education Association explored how to better help students "develop their power and equip them to assist in the rebuilding of our already profoundly disturbed national life." In response, it issued a report that included the assertions that "schools failed to give students an appreciation of their heritage as American citizens," and "our secondary schools did not prepare adequately for the responsibilities of community life." This report provided the impetus for the Eight Year Study, a school reform effort that sought to change the very nature and purpose of the secondary curriculum and experience. Creators of the Eight Year Study asserted that "the curriculum in every part should have one clear, major purpose. That purpose is to bring every young American his great heritage of freedom, to develop understanding of the kind of life we seek, and to inspire devotion to human welfare." Ambitious and in many ways groundbreaking research, the Study's influence was muted amidst the events of World War II.[29]

Many Americans resisted strongly the shift away from direct religious referents in ethical education. Rhetoric from the era of nineteenth-century common schools was revived by those whose appeals to nonsectarianism appear less genuine than those of nineteenth-century reformers. In his 1942 case for increased Bible reading and religious education in public schools, W. S. Fleming asked, "Can the parochial schools solve the problem of religion in education? Never. Even if all other churches followed suit and set up parochial schools there would still be in the sadly weakened public school the two-thirds of the children who never darken church doors, and from these would still come the dangerous elements we now have." He fumes over disputes such as which Bible version to use: "*While we strain out the gnat of sectarianism and swallow the camel of secularism in education, we prepare a poison potion that will kill the nation.* While we fuss, the devil is gloatingly getting America."[30]

These charges reflect the growing perception that national educational policy was becoming increasingly secular in its approach. We should be careful not to assume, however, that ethical education had fully separated from its colonial religious origins at the local level. The persistent gap between broader national policy and actual regional practice was clearly present in the relationship between religion and public schools. In the early twentieth century, conservative Protestants maintained significant control on the local level, particularly in the rural South—censoring textbooks, hiring and firing teachers based on their ideology, and supporting continued Bible reading, prayer, and religious ceremonies. Their influence did not extend to national organizations that influenced broader educational policy, however, and thus the overall shift away from religiously based ethical education continued. Interestingly, though, formal legalization of Bible reading actually *increased* in the first half of the twentieth century. But this seems less an indication of broad rising commitment to religiously based ethical education than what Tyack calls "a hardening of ideological arteries" by Protestants who "began to lose faith in persuasion and assimilative reform and moved instead to coercive reform through laws that would symbolize their dominance."[31]

One particular ideological issue that began to emerge for conservative religious groups in the twentieth century and continues to generate social, political, and legal controversy is the teaching of evolution. Although Darwin's *Origin of Species* was published in 1859, nineteenth-century theologians and scientists generally left one another alone. But with the advent of the *Scopes* trial in 1925, many religious Americans felt that their schools and their curricula threatened to betray long-standing beliefs about human origins and the primacy of religious doctrine. After science teacher John Scopes was convicted of violating a Tennessee state law that prohibited the teaching of evolution in public schools, a wave of other states introduced legislation to prohibit mention of evolution in textbooks, and publishers responded by adopting a calculated silence on the issue. It was not until the 1950s that science education, expanded dramatically in the wake of Sputnik, again engaged with the issue.[32]

In the two decades following *Scopes*, America's tradition of local discretion enabled compromise regarding religious-ethical instruction in the form of "released time." This system allowed students to attend religious classes in their own tradition for a few hours a week, and it enjoyed wide popularity, particularly in the 1940s. One parent became disenchanted with this religious instruction and, when her ten-year-old son was harassed for declining to participate, she ultimately filed suit. Her 1948 legal challenge in *McCollum v. Board of Education* resulted in the Supreme Court ruling it unconstitutional to have religious classes taught by religious instructors during school hours. In the majority decision, Justice Hugo Black repeated the Jeffersonian metaphor he had revived in an opinion he wrote just a year earlier:

> The First Amendment has erected a wall between Church and State which must be kept high and impregnable. Here not only are the State's tax-supported public school buildings used for the dissemination of religious doctrines. The State also affords sectarian groups an invaluable aid in that it helps to provide pupils for their religious classes through use of the State's compulsory public school machinery. This is not separation of Church and State.

Nationwide reaction to the decision was one of anger and defiance, with many churches and school districts claiming they would carry on their joint work in spite of the Court. While this was one of the first times when the judicial wall of separation leaned against majority sensibilities, it would certainly not be the last.[33]

THE EMERGING WALL OF SEPARATION

This image of "a wall of separation between church and state" has become a classic metaphor and legal concept in American judicial history, but the reality is far more complicated and compromised. As Ronald Thiemann observes with no small irony, "The day Justice Black penned those fateful words, the U.S. Supreme Court was convened with the invocation, 'God save this honorable court.' A few hundred yards across the Mall from the Supreme Court building, the two houses of Congress opened their sessions with prayers offered from chaplains supported by public funds and paid with currency inscribed with the motto, 'In God We Trust.'"[34]

This tension between legal judgments requiring greater separation and the actual religious traditions and practices of Americans existed powerfully in the post-World War II years. Jonathan Zimmerman points to a strong current of generalized religious faith that began to develop in American culture and politics during the late 1940s, including a wave of popular songs, movies, and even children's toys with religious themes. Connections between religious commitment and patriotic loyalty were also increasingly claimed and emphasized. In 1954, Congress voted to add the phrase "under God" to the Pledge of Allegiance to draw an overt contrast to the atheistic threat of communism; three years later, it passed a joint resolution declaring "In God We Trust" the official motto of the United States. A 1962 nationwide survey indicated that 42 percent of school systems included Bible reading without comment in their curricula. About one-third of public schools conducted daily devotional services, and at least five states authorized the Lord's Prayer in the classroom.[35]

Contrast this atmosphere with the landmark Supreme Court rulings of 1962 and 1963, which effectively prohibited school-directed prayer and Bible reading in the nation's public schools. *Engel v. Vitale* was prompted by the New York State Board of Regents' 1958 adoption of a specific prayer for use in New York classrooms: "Almighty God, we acknowledge our dependence upon Thee, and we beg Thy blessings upon us, our parents, our teachers, and our Country." The father of two Jewish boys, who were harassed for their refusal to participate, brought suit, and the Court responded with a quick and definitive decision. Justice Black wrote, "We think that the constitutional prohibition against laws respecting an establishment of religion must at least mean that in this country it is no part of the business of government to compose official prayers." The following year, the Court ruled on two consolidated cases concerning Bible reading and school prayer. In *Abington v. Schempp*, the Court banned all required prayer and Bible reading in public schools.[36]

Response to the *Engel* and *Schempp* decisions was largely one of massive disapproval across the country. While resistance was generally covert in the Northern states, the South openly denounced the decisions. Alabama Governor George Wallace issued a defiant plan to continue with Bible reading and prayer. Numerous attempts were made throughout the 1960s, both by legislative bodies and grassroots organizations, to restore prayer to the public schools. Many districts adopted a "moment of silence" instead. Historically, Catholic activists had sought to make the public schools as secular as possible, thus diminishing Protestant dominance. But in the wake of the *Engel* ruling, Catholic and even Jewish leaders expressed dismay that a "simple and voluntary declaration of belief in God by public school children" was being outlawed. They saw the efforts to remove all reference to God from schools as deeply troubling.[37]

Some religious groups, however, saw a silver lining in the *Engel* and *Schempp* decisions. In 1963 the Presbyterian Church (PCUSA) issued a statement that asserted that "Bible reading and prayers as devotional acts tend toward indoctrination or meaningless ritual and should be omitted for both reasons." As part of the shift away from an ethical education linked directly with the (dominant Protestant) religious framework, the religious elements had become increasingly less meaningful to the many students whose religious commitments (or lack thereof) lay elsewhere. While the resulting "culture religion" remained attractive to many religious liberals, at least some conservative adherents felt that an empty, uninspiring ethical education was worse than none at all.[38]

While the majority opinion on *Schempp* was clear in its rejection of devotional Bible reading, it also added an important emphasis on public schools' role in educating *about* religion:

> It might well be said that one's education is not complete without a study of comparative religion or the history of religion and its relationship to the advancement of civilization. It certainly may be said that the Bible is worthy of study for its literary and historic qualities. Nothing we have said here indicates that such study of the Bible or of religion, when presented objectively as part of a secular program of education, may not be effected consistently with the First Amendment.

While I will argue in later chapters that the idea of "objective study about religion" needs rethinking, this acknowledgment by the Court was one of the first judicial depictions of the government's role as one of *neutrality* regarding religion, as opposed to the heretofore prevailing idea of *separation* between government and religion. If the state via public education is to be neutral regarding religion, it must not only avoid favoring one religion over another but also avoid favoring nonreligion over religion. Separationist policies that seek to prevent religion from being explored in the context of public education create a decidedly non-neutral environment. But the implications of this conceptual distinction were not recognized, as ethical education continued to disengage from its singular religious source and transmuted into curricula that largely ignored or suppressed consideration of deep ethical sources almost entirely, religious and otherwise.[39]

ETHICAL EDUCATION ON THE SECULAR SIDE OF THE WALL

While post-World War II America expressed strong support for ethical education, this commitment began to wane in the 1960s, as a concern for maintaining moral neutrality gained priority along with stronger distinctions between the public and private realms. Added to this was an increasing focus on technological and scientific advancement that emphasized "academic" skills.

It was out of this decade, however, that two distinctive approaches to ethical education emerged. In 1966, the values clarification approach was introduced by Raths, Harmin, and Simon in their book *Values and Teaching: Working with Values in the Classroom.* While this approach has largely fallen out of favor, the sentiments behind it still operate as a subtext in many classrooms today. As its name suggests, the values clarification model aims for students to engage in discourse that allows them to clarify their own set of values through discussion of moral situations. In this approach, the teacher is encouraged to help students explore their own beliefs but not to provide direct instruction concerning their possible benefits and drawbacks.[40]

Although widely popular among teachers (one particular handbook sold an amazing 600,000 copies), values clarification came under harsh criticism beginning in the 1970s, both on empirical and conceptual grounds. From 1969 to 1985, a total of seventy-four research studies indicated that values clarification programs fostered very limited changes in a variety of moral categories: personal values, self-concept, attitudes toward school, dogmatism, and behavior. This preponderance of data did little to curtail the use of values clarification techniques in schools, however. It wasn't until philosophical and political critiques raised the specter of unchecked relativism that values clarification was widely abandoned.[41]

From a conceptual standpoint, Thomas Lickona criticizes values clarification for making no distinction between what one wants to do and what one ought to do. In his view, it makes the mistake of treating children like adults who only needed to clarify values that were already appropriate (assuming adults' values are appropriate!). He shares this telling episode from a values clarification lesson, in which a ninth-grade English teacher conducted a "values voting" exercise.

> She asked her students, "How many of you have ever shoplifted?" Most raised their hands. "Don't you think shoplifting is wrong?" the teacher asked (slipping momentarily from the prescribed neutrality). "We have a right to the material things in life," answered a student. Others nodded their agreement. "At that point I thought," the teacher says, "'Good grief, where do I go from here?' Thank God the bell rang."[42]

Values clarification as a structured curriculum is rare in American schools today, but many teachers, uncomfortable with the notion of prescribing specific morality for their students, end up encouraging—perhaps more in effect than intent—the opposite stance of moral subjectivism in classroom discussions of controversial issues.

The other distinctive approach to ethical education that emerged concurrently with values clarification was the highly influential cognitive-developmental model proposed by Lawrence Kohlberg. Through the discussion of moral dilemmas such as the Heinz vignette, Kohlberg argued, students could advance through the various stages of moral reasoning and judgment he had identified. While some research suggests that classroom dilemma discussion improves moral reasoning capacities in students, this raises the question of whether the capacities measured are ultimately significant in real-life moral and ethical dilemmas. Critics have charged that these hypothetical vignettes are too contrived and simplistic, lacking the complexity that people must navigate in their actual ethical lives. Students are asked to make zero-sum choices without the possibility of reinterpreting or reconceptualizing either the situation or the response options. Other detractors argue that these dilemmas are too decontextualized, and that Kohlberg's moral stages are too heavily weighted toward abstract reasoning rather than interpersonal understanding and care.[43]

Much of original Kohlbergian theory has been revised or discredited, but its legacy remains in some programs that overemphasize a highly individualistic, Manichaean orientation to moral conflict. In the view of some critics, this approach often short-circuits the deliberative process. For example, Daniel Pekarsky observes that "the choice-situation as understood by Kohlberg is a very late phase of the process of deliberation" and should occur only after a process of articulating the conflict and attempting to dissolve it through dialogue. In a similar vein, others point out that group processes often involved in moral decisions are neglected in Kohlbergian theory. Kohlberg himself eventually recognized the limitations of his original model's narrow cognitive focus and began to emphasize a more comprehensive approach involving the fostering of democratic school community to encourage ethical growth.[44]

Developed in part as a response to the moral ambiguity of values clarification, the character education model that began to emerge in the late 1980s is by far the most popular approach to ethical education in schools today. Anchored in an Aristotelian notion of moral habituation, character education efforts typically rest on an assumption of core virtues held in common across cultural and religious differences. On first glance, this focus might give the impression that deeper ethical sources such as religion are explored in conjunction with these virtues. But the agenda here is generality rather than particularity, and thus depth is avoided. As Thomas Lickona, a leading proponent of character education, asserts, "People of all religious faiths and people of no religious faith can agree that moral and intellectual virtues are the rational foundation of a civil society and the basis of good character." Even if we grant this debatable contention (many fundamentalist faiths, for example, are quite suspect of intellectual virtues with wholly rational foundations)—and even if we accept a particular list of core virtues (common ones include respect, caring, justice, and citizenship)—we are left with enormous disagreement about what these virtues mean in different contexts. For example, consider the ongoing battles over welfare policy—some say caring means providing only job training and child care, others say direct financial assistance is an ethical obligation, and so on. To the extent that character education avoids these complexities (which it usually does), it remains a radically incomplete approach to ethical education in schools.[45]

Character education is often portrayed by its critics as being consistently superficial; Alfie Kohn criticizes its typical "value of the month" approach, with each value examined singly and often out of context. Warren Nord concurs:

> No matter how philosophically sophisticated its advocates might be, in practice character education tends to be intellectually superficial, in part, at least, because it emphasizes consensus and training. It doesn't deal well with questions of deep justification—those existential, philosophical, and religious questions about the human condition, the

nature of morality, and the worldviews that make sense of, and ground, consensus moral virtues and values—because they are, after all, controversial. Moreover, character education programs tend to emphasize personal morality and deemphasize those social, ideological, and institutional dimensions of our moral life that complicate moral decision making and are controversial.

This relative lack of attention to broader, societal structures contributing to injustice is a flaw emphasized by other social critics as well. One of character education's primary attractions to school districts seems to be its straightforward, precept-friendly approach; this simplicity, however, cannot accommodate the complex interplay of personal choices and the social setting within which we make them. Besides underemphasizing ethical complexity, the typical character education model of fixed, pre-identified virtues also limits opportunity for ethical discourse. At least to some extent, the opportunity to deliberate about the merits of specific virtues—particularly those sometimes in tension with one another, such as honesty and kindness—and the possibility of reasonable alternatives is an important step in learning to apply moral commitments to new situations. In addition (as I will explore more fully in chapter 5), the opportunity for dissent and revision is a vital element in communicating across ethical differences. Without practicing such deliberative skills, students—and society—are left with ignorant tolerance or intolerance as their only options.[46]

As with most forms of ethical education, the empirical record on character education is unconvincing at best. Many scholars describe the research base as shallow, frequently accusing the character education movement in particular of paying little attention to complicated variables: what works in which settings with what students? And what would it mean that character education "works" anyway? For instance, the coeditors of the journal *Character Education*, in identifying "appropriate data on measurable changes in key variables" for program evaluation, list questions such as "Have absences decreased? Are office referrals down? Do more students make the honor roll?" While certainly not meaningless information, answers to such questions hardly constitute a comprehensive evaluation of ethical growth in students. Such a focus reveals a typical concern of character education with social convention and obedience; learning to engage with a diversity of ethical perspectives and nurture mutual understanding and respect seem beyond the scope of much character education curricula.[47]

FROM ENTANGLEMENT TO ENGAGEMENT

Ethical education in the United States prior to the 1960s was a legal, political, and moral failure. On a legal level, judicial challenges resulted in courts affirming a view of disestablishment that justly criticized the dominance of a pan-Protestant ethos in public schools. On a political level, schools and governments became rightly sensitive to the growing political voice of religious and ethnic minorities. And most fundamentally, on a moral level, a tyranny of the majority in which a single version of the good life is foisted upon minorities who reasonably believe otherwise is morally oppressive.

For these reasons, the shift away from a singular Protestant-dominated ethical education over the course of our nation's history has been justified. But in pulling away from a single ethical source, school curricula have suppressed consideration of deep ethical sources almost entirely, both religious and otherwise. In particular, today's character education offers a superficial, virtue-oriented approach that overlooks substantive differences among belief systems and the role of context in moral reasoning. In summary, the effort to address morality in *abstraction* from deeper ethical sources has *also* failed.

As I mentioned at the outset of this chapter, it seems likely that some localities continue to rely on the singular ethical source of Protestant Christianity, state regulations and judicial rulings notwithstanding. Even for communities that have insulated themselves from this historic shift from entanglement to separation, the type of ethical education I advocate in this book involves a deeply significant change in curriculum and pedagogy. Our public square and its citizenry need a better vision, one that avoids both separation and entanglement.

The public school emphasis on avoiding entanglement with religion emerged from a 1971 Supreme Court ruling that described a three-part test for legally sufficient separation of church and state: "First, the statute must have a secular legislative purpose; second, its principal or primary effect must be one that neither advances nor inhibits religion; finally, the statute must not foster an excessive entanglement with religion."[48] This set of conditions became known as the "Lemon test," and would be used in many cases to follow, especially school funding challenges. The validity of this final criterion involving "excessive entanglement" continues to be debated by both legal scholars and the Supreme Court justices themselves, however, and for good reason.

While the negative connotation of "entanglement"—in the form of ethical education dominated by a singular religious source—is certainly unacceptable, our educational response should not be one of separation but of *engagement*. Our public schools should actively engage with religious and other deep ethical sources in order to foster the capacity to hold informed, respectful discourse across ethical difference. If by entanglement our judiciary means "complicated ethical disagreement," then the Lemon test *should* be discarded. We would do well to remember the Court's opinion three years before *Lemon* even appeared:

> Any word spoken, in class, in the lunchroom, or on the campus, that deviates from the view of another person may start an argument or cause a disturbance. But our Constitution says we must take this risk, and our history says that it is this sort of hazardous freedom—this kind of openness—that is the basis of our national strength and of the independence and vigor of Americans who grow up and live in this relatively permissive, often disputatious, society.

Some judicial analysts now suggest that the courts have already begun a process of moving away from a policy of separation of church and state to one of neutrality. They cite numerous recent Supreme Court decisions that are far more tolerant of religious expression and that seek to strike a tenuous balance between neither favoring nor disfavoring religion.[49] But this is not enough; simply put, I believe our public schools and society need more than neutrality regarding religion and other deep ethical sources—they require *engagement*.

This argument is not simply a call for including a broad array of ethical perspectives. By the 1980s, the strategy of conservative Christians had shifted from advocating a return to God-centered schools toward a multicultural strategy of insisting on "equal time" for their views. But Jonathan Zimmerman sees this route as a curricular dead end: unlike the relatively simpler approach of adding more cultural information to textbooks to appease other multicultural interest groups, "different moral frameworks cannot be mixed into the curriculum like so many spices, enhancing its overall flavor." Zimmerman argues that "these frameworks are fundamentally 'incommensurable'—that is, each one presupposes the invalidity of the other. In this they differ sharply from racial and ethnic claims upon the history curriculum, which have generally been folded into a single overarching story."[50]

I am not advocating the type of laundry-list, additive approach that Zimmerman describes, as I hope to make clear in the following chapters. But neither can we respond to the reality of ethical difference by labeling beliefs incommensurable and walling them off from our public school curricula. This serves only to hinder our civic capacity to both learn from one another and live together respectfully, whether in agreement or disagreement. Schools and curricula that avoid substantive exploration of ethical disagreement betray whatever commitments to mutual respect they proclaim. As I will argue in chapter 3, genuine respect in fact *requires* such exploration; without significant educational efforts toward understanding the sources of our deep ethical disagreements, we fail to respect one another and thus weaken public schools' commitment to the common good.

The American public school, from its origins in the mid-nineteenth century through today, has been a flash point for our national and local struggles to decide how to live together. In this chapter I have barely touched upon the historical dispute over evolution and have not even mentioned similar, ongoing controversies regarding sex education, textbook content and selection, library censorship, and anti-drug abuse education. All of these controversies represent our unending, inevitable disputes over visions of the good life. Clearly the relationships between religion, politics, and education are tremendously complex and undeniably threatening. But the twentieth-century legal shift to separation has not been and cannot be the answer. As Robert Michaelsen observes:

> The relentless logic of separation turns, like a vortex, ever in upon itself. It is an attractive logic—neat, sharp, decisive, pure. It is also a fateful logic which can only lead in its conclusion to the complete separation of religion from public life. The merits of such a result are arguable; the possibility of its achievement in the United States remote. Much as the mind of logic might wish to articulate a clear-cut principle for encompassing relationships between religion and the state, American community experience will not be so easily encompassed.[51]

Rather than pursuing this attractive but ill-advised logic of separation, our increasingly diverse society and the schools it supports (and in turn is supported by) need to recognize the virtue and necessity of ethical engagement. The following chapter will present an argument for why such engagement is essential if our liberal democracy's foundational principle of mutual respect is to be honored.

3

Why Religion Belongs
in Ethical Dialogue

Let's return for a moment to the *Brave New World* classroom discussion I described in the book's opening pages. Cheryl's assertion that "we shouldn't play God" was not merely a newly developing opinion or the result of a contrary mood—rather, it emerged from an *ethical framework*. As I will explain in more detail later in the chapter, we all have an underlying structure or framework to our lives that reflects our sense of what we value and pursue in life. This ethical framework helps orient and guide our lives, as well as shape our sense of identity.

My central claim in this chapter is that in many ethical controversies, mutual respect obligates us to strive to understand the ethical frameworks of those with whom we disagree. While the *Brave New World* discussion in my English class addressed hypothetical technology, versions of Cheryl's perspective are forwarded in similar controversies today, many with direct policy implications for how we live our lives together. For many opponents of stem cell research, their line of argument emerges from a religious-ethical framework. If I were to reject such an argument without striving to understand how their vision of God and virtue has shaped their position—viewing the harvesting of embryos as akin to abortion, for instance, and thus deeply immoral—I have not shown them respect.

For those readers concerned primarily with the application of Ethical Dialogue in the classroom, be forewarned that the first three sections of this chapter present a fairly abstract philosophical argument that may seem of little direct relevance to curriculum and pedagogy. My intent is to make the case that engaging with religious perspectives as a part of Ethical Dialogue is a matter of mutual respect, and thus an essential component of citizenship in any good society. The latter half of the chapter then offers a more concrete analysis of why religiously-informed ethical frameworks deserve significant attention in our public schools.

The basic theoretical argument of the chapter unfolds as follows:

1. Mutual respect is a vital feature of any good society.
2. Amidst ethical conflict, mutual respect requires that we strive to understand others' ethical frameworks.
3. Many people's ethical frameworks are deeply informed by religion.
4. Ethical Dialogue will often need to foster understanding of religious perspectives.

Much of current ethical education, in practice if not in theory, presumes the detachment of ethical and religious identity. Dialogue amidst these conditions of (at best) ignorant tolerance fails to understand the diverse ethical perspectives of students and thus fails to respect students themselves. It also fails to prepare *all* students to be citizens able to engage thoughtfully and productively with ethical disagreement in our pluralistic society. Our students and our society deserve and require better.

MUTUAL RESPECT AS A FOUNDATION FOR ETHICAL DIALOGUE

The starting assumption for this chapter is that a good society depends in part on people living in mutual respect. The argument for Ethical Dialogue also rests on this foundational premise that we owe respect to others as persons. If we endorse this idea, it naturally raises the question, "Well, what then does respect for others entail?" In order to answer this, we must begin a bit farther back and ask, "What is it about our status as humans that merits respect in the first place?" Stephen Darwall responds by suggesting a dual notion of respect: recognition respect and appraisal respect. The latter is what we usually mean when we say someone deserves our respect; we evaluate and commend features or characteristics of a person, such as honesty or generosity. In contrast, recognition respect doesn't measure a person but instead acknowledges that the fact that she simply is a person gives her a particular moral status.[1]

Recognition respect emphasizes the incommensurable worth of others. It is an egalitarian attitude that, unlike appraisal respect, makes no distinction based on merit. It is the respect owed to (all) others as equals. This universal emphasis resembles a Kantian version of mutual respect, where each person is treated as an instance of the universal and thus accorded respect simply by virtue of her personhood. While the egalitarian nature of recognition or universal respect is vital, such a conception alone is insufficient, because none of us are mere instances of the universal. Rather, we are particular individuals whose very uniqueness contributes to our worth and hence the respect we are owed.

What we need is a conception of respect for persons that integrates the universal unconditionality of Kantian respect with one more attentive to human particularity and personal identity. One promising possibility is offered by Loren Lomasky, who points to humans' natural pursuit of "projects" as a foundational rationale for mutual respect. He describes projects as the ends of human actions that "reach indefinitely into the future, play a central role within the ongoing endeavors of the individual, and provide a significant degree of structural stability to an individual's life."[2] Projects are, in a sense, a narrative structure. Some projects address external states of affairs in our lives, such as a goal to help cure cancer. Others focus on the kind of person one wishes to be, for instance, someone who values a happy family life over career advancement. While our various projects generally have some sort of internal consistency, this human characteristic of project pursuit need not involve some sort of fixed, fully rational "master plan."

The status of humans as project pursuers provides this integrated notion of respect we seek, one that includes both impersonal and personal considerations. It is impersonal in its applicability to everyone, but personal in that ultimate value resides in the particularity of each project pursuer. Gregory Vlastos suggests the image of parental love to analogize the relationship between universal respect and attention to individuality. A parent properly loves his or her child unconditionally, but this love manifests through an intimate understanding of the child's individuality; a love missing either facet would be found somehow wanting.[3]

Similarly, we cannot merely respect people in the abstract but must often be attentive to their particular identity. This identity might consist of a variety of influences: ethnic, religious, family history, and so on. In this regard, the often well-intentioned teacher who claims not to see his students' ethnicity but sees them as "just children" is actually neglecting a vital facet of respect. In addition, respect for particularity—for what people count as most significant about themselves—suggests the need for seeing others in part as they see themselves. The universal respect we owe others finds its locus of value in the particularity of individuals as project pursuers.

We should note that the broader Kantian conception is not left behind, however. The emphasis on personal uniqueness, the individuality of our projects and the specificity of our social location (often a major emphasis of "identity politics"), can be carried to an extreme that seeks to deny any common basis for moral reasoning. Our projects vary widely, and our social experiences generate perspectives that others do not share, but nevertheless we all have projects and we all navigate social space. Our social roles may shape our projects in deeply significant ways, but we ought not regard others entirely in terms of the roles they occupy. Our equal status as project pursuers should not be overwhelmed by the need to recognize and understand our particularities.

UNDERSTANDING AS VITAL FOR RESPECT

So far I have made the case that respect requires that we strive to understand other people's projects, what guides and gives shape to their lives. This requirement, however, is dependent upon context. Here, Lomasky's notion of humans as project pursuers can help illuminate the contextual link between mutual respect and understanding. In some interpersonal circumstances, we have a familiar and implicit understanding of others' projects, at least to the extent that is necessary for respectful interaction. But on a civic level, this familiarity cannot be assumed. In a diverse society, our projects—what counts as significant about who we are—will vary widely. To merely acknowledge that these projects vary, however, without seeking a deeper understanding of their particularities, produces a civic realm marked by ignorant tolerance or intolerance.

To illustrate the contextual requirements of respect, consider the issue first at an individual level. "Do I have to understand someone's projects in order to respect her?" the objection might begin. "Surely I can respect people—acquaintances, even strangers—without such deep understanding! If not, there aren't going to be too many people I truly respect." In response, we should recall that this thick notion of respect merges universal and particularistic elements. Much like Darwall's recognition respect, the universal requirements of respect—recognizing the humanity we all share and the obligations of tolerance it invokes—can and ought to exist between strangers as well as soul mates.

So while this universal respect for others is a baseline constant, the requirements of respect I have described in terms of project recognition exist on a continuum, determined by social context. The requirements of respect, for instance, rise significantly in situations of conflict, especially when freedom is at stake. Ordinary, low-stake interactions with strangers, such as paying for groceries or giving directions, do not carry extensive requirements of respect and thus deeper understanding. Even the acknowledgment of someone's right to worship according to his own religious tradition, for instance, is a generally accepted notion in American society; the respect involved here doesn't usually require understanding of particular traditions. But if I sought to *restrict* a particular form of worship (refusing to sanction work breaks for my employee to pray at appointed hours, for instance, where praying at those hours was required within the employee's religious community), the context introduces significantly greater requirements for mutual understanding if respect is to be realized between us.

But what about the many relationships we characterize as significant and enjoying more than universal respect, an objector might persist, but have never included a deliberate exploration of one another's projects? Is this assumed deeper respect merely illusory? Here it is important to recognize that people may interact using similar ethical conceptions while never explicitly voicing them. This would explain why I can interact with many professional colleagues in an atmosphere of significant mutual respect without us having explicitly considered one another's ethical sources. Total harmony is far from assumed here, however; just because I share with my teaching colleague general support for autonomy in adolescents doesn't mean we won't someday find ourselves in serious conflict over the appropriate response when one of our students engages in self-destructive behavior. At this juncture we will need to understand each other's ethical projects more fully if mutual respect is to be maintained. A sign of disrespect would be if I disagreed vehemently with my colleague but made no effort to understand the ethical perspective that informed his position.

Now let's extend these examples of individual interactions to a civic level. The previous illustrations suggest that low-stake interactions can occur with little effort toward understanding others' particularities, thanks to assumed ethical commonalities (e.g., I will pay the cashier what he says I owe, or I will give driving directions to the best of my knowledge). The sustaining bulwark of common ethical commitments thins dramatically, however, in our broader American civic society. This is not to say that most Americans do not share many assumptions about moral obligation—character education advocates are fond of pointing to a commonly recognized core of values, such as caring, honesty, fairness, responsibility, and respect for self and others. But the distinction between moral obligation and the broader ethical commitments that inform them is crucial here; the value of responsibility, for instance, makes sense only within a broader ethical framework that addresses questions such as "For whom am I responsible, and under what circumstances, and why?" So on a civic level, for example, while most citizens would share the value of caring for the poor, the ensuing public policy choices are at least as plentiful as the many visions of the good life that people in our society hold.

UNDERSTANDING PROJECTS INVOLVES EVALUATING THEM

Here it is important to point out that seeking to understand someone's project pursuit—the appraisal side of respect—necessarily involves a level of evaluation. In this sense, I cannot adequately respect someone's projects without evaluating them. In fact, an attitude of unexamined acceptance can often indicate a *lack* of respect—I don't care enough to do the hard work of understanding why you believe what you do, so I'll just put up with it (and you) as long as it doesn't impinge on my own projects.

It is vital to distinguish the *process* of evaluation from the *outcome*. Appraisal respect requires that we take other ethical projects seriously enough to investigate and consider their values when the context demands; it does not require that we ultimately agree with their substance. Put in terms of project pursuit, our respect for others is based on recognition of the particularity of others' projects, not endorsement of the specific nature of the projects themselves. (Here is where recognition respect and appraisal respect weave together; we recognize and thus respect others as project pursuers but then—when context warrants—complete that respect through our appraisal of the value of those projects.) Accordingly, we can respect others as project pursuers while ultimately disapproving of some of their projects.

For example, respect requires that I give a full hearing to the parents and student who request an alternative classroom text, one more congenial to their religious beliefs. It may even necessitate forbearance on my part that includes both my disapproval of their "project" and my willingness to accommodate them nonetheless. If I determine that their request entails disrespect for others' projects—for example, demanding that everyone use their proselytizing text—then I might reasonably reject their request (i.e., refuse to tolerate), but this outcome doesn't mean I haven't shown them respect. Indeed, an indiscriminate acceptance of widely conflicting projects would often result in an incoherent ethical system in which respect is actually shown to none of them. I cannot approve of an ethical project based on racial superiority, for example, while also endorsing universal human rights. As discussed in chapter 2, this susceptibility to uncritical acceptance of moral choices is a troubling flaw of much values clarification pedagogy.

A noteworthy but complicating corollary here is that respect need not be recognized by its recipient as respect. This seems particularly salient in situations where the understanding we gain of another leads not to greater acceptance but rather to refusal to tolerate his ethical framework or at least its manifestations in his actions. Such refusal will likely be inaccurately perceived by this person as disrespect but, as I have argued, the evaluative outcome does not determine whether respect has been given. Additionally, although evaluative criteria are often quite complex, this should not leave us resigned to a subjectivism in which respect is purely a matter of individual perception. It is certainly possible, however, that my process of evaluation might suffer from misinterpretation, even when undertaken with the best of motivations. But the notion of misinterpretation only makes sense, of course, if criteria for evaluation do in fact exist. To insist otherwise is to concede that anyone's critique of another's ethical project—and anyone's ethical project itself—is beyond reproach or error. The end point of this position is a moral subjectivism that precludes moral judgment of any kind. In chapter 5 I will explore the complexities and challenges of such deliberation in further detail.

RESPECTFUL UNDERSTANDING AS A MORAL, NOT INSTRUMENTAL, CLAIM

My goal so far in this chapter has been to develop the idea that Ethical Dialogue, as a matter of mutual respect, will frequently need to involve efforts toward understanding conflicting ethical frameworks. But why do we even need a moral theory of respect to undergird a case for Ethical Dialogue? That is, why does an education aimed at developing a capacity for mutual understanding and thoughtful public deliberation require normative claims about the inherent value of respect for others? Couldn't the more instrumental case be made that Ethical Dialogue contributes to a more democratic society, that improved mutual understanding helps us make better decisions about how to live together?

Some evidence does suggest the value of perspective taking in improving interpersonal relationships, but how this affects our ability to reason together remains unclear.[4] The instrumental argument might also hold that the understanding generated by mutual respect is a necessary component of any genuinely dialogical engagement; that is, we cannot engage in productive dialogue without understanding one another's position. Furthermore, the deliberative process itself—if it is to be more than a thin disguise for simple adversarial politics—requires a forum wherein participants share respect and equal standing. The frequent absence of these conditions, in fact, is one of the most powerful criticisms against deliberative democratic theory. Indeed, a central contention of this book is that the capacity for mutual respect and understanding required for genuine deliberation is a virtue that needs to be learned—hence the need for ethical education.

But the value of mutual respect goes far deeper than its utility in providing the means for effective and justice-promoting deliberation. My claim here is that mutual respect is not merely instrumental in the pursuit of the common good, but partly *constitutive* of it. To the extent that we do not respect others as project pursuers—and thus seek to understand their projects—we have neglected what is good in and of itself. There is no common good with mere tolerance.

Some theorists argue that critics of "mere" tolerance are not sufficiently appreciative of its value in light of historical oppression of ethical difference. But I contend that an "agreement to disagree" absent any real understanding of other points of view—while sometimes the best we can do—hardly serves as a fitting educational vision for our schools and our children. Certainly an absence of tolerance—a *modus vivendi* of individual goods constrained by instrumental truce, for instance—cannot claim to support a common good. But even a genuine moral tolerance along the lines of Rawls's constitutional consensus provides only a limited set of moral-political restraints as its highest value; the moral equality of all persons is not a substantive ideal, and thus the common good of just community cannot be fully realized. The value of mutual respect, while generally supported by its role in encouraging understanding and thoughtful deliberation, stands self-sufficiently as a normative claim about how human beings should live together.[5]

The Link between Project Pursuit and Broader Ethical Frameworks

At the beginning of this chapter, I suggested that behind Cheryl's assertion that "we shouldn't play God" was an ethical framework, a broad notion of the good life that informed her values, her commitments, and—in this chapter's terminology—her projects. In many cases, then, respecting the particularity of someone's projects will require an understanding of the ethical framework from which those projects emerge.

We all have ethical frameworks, and they help shape who we are. We cannot do without them—if we claim to know where we stand on matters of importance to us, we have an ethical framework. Combined with our life experiences, they help shape our sense of self. Charles Taylor uses the term *narrative* to describe the way our identities are shaped over time by a range of experiences and beliefs. He explains, "In order to have a sense of who we are, we have to have a notion of how we have become, and of where we are going. . . . My life always has this degree of narrative understanding, that I understand my present action in the form of an 'and then': there was A (what I am), and then I do B (what I project to become)." In this way, understanding both the self and its location require a recognition of what came before, what has shaped who we are, and our relationship to the good we seek.[6]

While the notion of narrative is a particularly evocative one, this shouldn't be taken as merely a string of experiences that add up to a particular self. The self is not simply a series of attachments or evaluations. Rather, the various identifications that arise over a life's course contribute to a broader framework within which we stand to evaluate the world around us, a framework whose significance is more than the sum of its parts.[7] This also speaks to the complexity of the self and again raises the question of how fully we can understand others' unfamiliar ethical frameworks, a challenge I will return to in chapter 4.

Our selves, then, are inextricably linked with—and in many ways defined by—our various ethical projects as they comprise a broader framework. I use "ethical" here to distinguish it from the range of more trivial commitments that fill our lives—picking up the dry cleaning, for instance, or that cell phone contract we foolishly signed. Other commitments that we might consider rather humdrum, however—homeroom parent, city council member, and so on—may in fact point toward significant ethical beliefs, such as a determination to be deeply involved in our child's education or a conviction that we owe service to our community.

In the context of deep ethical conflict, to genuinely respect someone—to strive to understand her identity—we need as full a picture as possible of her ethical framework, the horizon within which she moves and chooses and lives. This horizon often extends beyond that individual's actions and choices, however, and includes relationships to broader social communities. Perhaps most commonly an ethnic or religious affiliation, multiple communal identifications often exist within the same individual (think, for instance, of a self-described Chicana, whose gender and ethnic affiliations significantly shape her identity). These webs of connection are frequently deemphasized by modern culture, which privileges the notion of a detached, independent self. But to ignore the relevance of these social factors is to overlook a vital influence on people's ethical frameworks.

THE IMPLICATIONS FOR CURRICULA AND PEDAGOGY

The educational implications of these requirements for respect are clearly significant. The importance of offering universal respect to others, while seeking to understand and accommodate their ethical particularities, is a central theme here as well as in broader multicultural theory and curricula. With these expectations in mind, the cognitive, empathic, and deliberative bar for Ethical Dialogue can seem dauntingly high. It requires an approach to education that, while seeking to explore a range of ethical perspectives, values depth over breadth. As Thomas Hill Jr. contends, "To study a wide range of cultures superficially, like sampling many dishes at a smorgasbord, may be personally rewarding, but is unlikely to contribute significantly to overcoming the problems of cross-cultural misunderstanding and disrespect."[8]

Yet this seems to be the most common pedagogical approach in our K–12 schools, a thin sampling of many perspectives but little commitment to grappling with the challenges that such diversity presents. Unless we understand the ethical frameworks that inform our deliberation about living together in society, we have not met the requirements of respect. Granted, this understanding will never be complete, but certainly a vast and significant expanse exists between willful ignorance of another's projects and first-person understanding. It is the movement from the former toward the latter that ethical education should foster, thus helping us fulfill our foundational obligation to demonstrate respect toward others.

I have argued here that in circumstances of ethical controversy, mutual understanding of others' ethical frameworks is a vital element of respect. As I acknowledged previously, the contextual nature of this requirement means that such understanding is not always necessary for respect to be demonstrated. But when deep ethical conflict *does* exist, mutual understanding fosters awareness of others' interests we are obligated to respect. It is important to note, however, that mutual understanding is not an entirely *sufficient* element of respect either. My understanding of why a particular ethical framework places great value in a certain religious observance means little, for instance, if I conclude that because *I* don't share that belief, it should bear no weight in our deliberations about how to live together. Respect often requires mutual understanding, but always requires more as well.

Ethical Dialogue—and the conception of respect that undergirds it—represents a significant departure from typical ethical education, as my critique toward the end of chapter 2 suggests. Both the overly narrow focus of "morality as obligation" curricula and the vague, decontextualized programs of much "character education" do little to address the complexity of our particular ethical selves, and thus fail to foster the depth of understanding that mutual respect requires.

Moral education concerned solely with obligation and behavior is most clearly in conflict with Ethical Dialogue. Structurally, a "thin" approach that seeks to affirm a universalistic moral core while denying its dependence on deeper ethical sources provides little justification for our behavior beyond instrumental convenience. Such a foundation hardly proves sufficient for an ethic of justice or care that generally serves as the moral core. As Eamonn Callan argues:

> Given that the thin ethical concepts are parasitic on the thick ones, a program of moral education such as Kohlberg's, which takes justice as its governing concept while claiming to discount the "bag of virtues," must be worse than misguided; it must be incoherent, because justice is

virtually bereft of meaning when torn from its background in an array of thick ethical concepts. Without that background, the use of thin concepts can be little more than pure caprice.[9]

While Kohlberg's original, strictly rationalist approaches to moral education have been largely abandoned, the emphasis on a universalistic moral core continues in much psychological research and the curricula it generates.[10]

Besides its structural weakness, the focus on obligation and behavior leaves us with a thin veneer of moral obligation that fails to resonate with many students whose own frameworks are inspired by far richer and more varied sources. In many instances, teachers are forced to actively sidestep these sources, as I did when Cheryl suggested that humans should not usurp God's role as creator. The procedural rationality that remains when ethical sources are ignored is inadequate for students whose personal narratives include a range of influences, religious or otherwise. Universal precepts—whose status as the lowest common denominator serves as their primary justification—are by themselves insufficient for robust ethical dialogue. While political deliberation often requires citizens to seek common ground (a point I develop at length in chapter 5), this ground cannot be reached through a deliberate ignorance of others' beliefs and experiences.

Character education, on the other hand, with its focus on "core virtues," might be seen as escaping a critique that emphasizes the centrality of strong ethical sources. In fact, its detractors sometimes criticize modern character education because of its explicit endorsement of certain virtues and their implicit links to dominant religious sources. Character education advocates generally respond, however, that such virtues are common to all humanity and transcend religious and cultural differences. But this philosophy—and especially its implementation in practice—neglects a concern for particularity. Simply insisting that we "all" share such standards will hardly make those standards students' own, at least in ways that will enable them to navigate the myriad ethical contexts of their lives.

What *are* the sources for students' rich and varied ethical frameworks? At the broadest level of response, we can point to whatever culture(s) surround them. In the parlance of multicultural education, "ethnic" is usually the assumed modifier when "culture" is used. Indeed, the role of ethnicity is undoubtedly salient in the formation of students' ethical identities, although comprehensive visions of "the good life" generally play a more auxiliary role. Some ethnic identifications, however, may serve as a primary ethical source (e.g., Afrocentrism). But even for frameworks that emerge from sources other than religious, they generally take on a function analogous to religion in an individual's life. As a result, the process of Ethical Dialogue involves many of the same considerations, regardless of whether the framework can be explicitly identified as religious; in the next section I address this issue as it relates to the notion of "secular worldviews."

RELIGIOUS FRAMEWORKS AND SECULAR WORLDVIEWS: IS THERE A DIFFERENCE?

Is there something about religion that sets it apart from other ethical frameworks? Besides the rare occasion when religion is a direct topic of study in public schools, religion seems most likely to enter classroom dialogue around broad ethical questions: What does it mean to be human? What does it mean to be good? What type of life should I lead? Certainly such questions are a primary concern of many religions. Yet answers to— or at least reflections on—these questions are only part of religion. Despite the Western philosophical overemphasis on "doctrine," the terrain of religion also generally includes communities, cultures, traditions, and rituals that are not adequately addressed when religious beliefs and their relation to metaphysical questions are the sole focus. To the extent that these other characteristics are present and influential in the shape of religious adherents' ethical frameworks, they deserve consideration in ethical education. Dialogue that does not recognize these various commitments in participants will result in an inadequate understanding of their ethical frameworks.

For public schoolteachers, understandably wary of violating church-state boundaries, the *legal* definition of religion is likely of greater concern than theoretical distinctions. The U.S. Supreme Court has offered a vague definition of religion. In 1968, *United States v. Seeger* included the ruling that religious conviction is not defined as belief in a "Supreme Being" but "whether a given belief that is sincere and meaningful occupies a place in the life of its possessor parallel to that filled by the orthodox belief in God." The conception of religion established in *Seeger* was further elaborated in *Welsh v. United States* (1970), which emphasized that military exemption "is not limited to those whose opposition to war is prompted by orthodox or parochial religious beliefs. A registrant's conscientious objection to all war is 'religious' within the meaning of [the statute] if this opposition stems from the registrant's moral, ethical, or religious beliefs about what is right and wrong and these beliefs are held with the strength of traditional religious convictions." This ruling further clarified that God need not be a part of the belief, just something analogous to belief in God.[11]

It appears, then, that robust ethical frameworks not traditionally considered religious nevertheless have legal standing akin to religious belief. But legal complexity remains, such as with avowedly secular beliefs that reach ultimacy in a believer's life (e.g., communism); theologian Paul Tillich terms these "quasi-religions." Some, such as the plaintiffs in the Sixth Circuit case *Mozert v. Hawkins County Board of Education* (1987), argue that secular humanism falls into this seemingly oxymoronic category of secular-religious belief. In a recent example of this legal confusion, public charter Waldorf schools in California were accused of promoting religion through the influence of anthroposophy, a philosophy created by the original founder of Waldorf schools, Rudolph Steiner. This belief system rests on the conviction that human intellect can contact spiritual worlds, and some parents have accused these public Waldorf schools of weaving this belief into the school curricula. School officials responded that anthroposophy, without a "priesthood or dogma," isn't a religion. A federal court initially dismissed the case, but the Ninth U.S. Circuit Court of Appeals reinstated the lawsuit two years later, underscoring our judicial ambivalence. In 2005, the court again ruled in favor of the Waldorf schools.[12]

One way in which some theorists have sought to avoid the definitional question is to use the overarching term *worldview*. This strategy acknowledges that while conventional religious belief is most often associated with various conceptions of the good around which people shape their lives, it is important to recognize that many secular conceptions of the good exist that also serve life-shaping functions. Whether secular or religious in nature, these frameworks seek to address deep, existential questions of meaning: How should I live my life? What is important to value? What are my obligations to others—family, friends, strangers? Some conceptions of the good are more comprehensive than others, but each offers a view of the world from which implications can be drawn concerning how one should live. Some of these more secular worldviews aren't easily named but emerge from a host of "isms" such as naturalism, humanism, materialism, consumerism, pacifism, socialism, and behaviorism.

I find the notion of worldview useful, up to a point. Religion generally involves a comprehensive conception of the good, a robust and pervasive ethical framework; many of the "isms" promote a particular conception of the good, but their domain is more limited.[13] So while religion may reasonably fall under the broader umbrella term of worldview, it often has characteristics that secular worldviews do not share. Nevertheless, given that many ethical questions—and arguably full ethical frameworks themselves—are informed by nonreligious sources, one might wonder whether this book's ultimate focus on religious-ethical frameworks generates an arbitrary exclusion of secular worldviews from exploration. *No such exclusion, arbitrary or otherwise, of secular ethical frameworks should occur in Ethical Dialogue.* The characteristics of religion I have mentioned are not intended to be used as a template for including or excluding ethical frameworks from consideration. Whether a particular framework as a whole qualifies as a religion is somewhat beside the point for Ethical Dialogue.

One particularly useful by-product of recognizing that secular worldviews promote their own conceptions of the good is that we can avoid the mistake of assuming that nonreligious ethical frameworks are somehow less partisan than religious ones. "Secular" frameworks should not be equated with "neutral" frameworks any more than my students' argument that medical research is an unmitigated good would qualify as a neutral position on stem cell research. Visions of the good life are not restricted to religious frameworks, of course. Secular ethical frameworks that offer a robust vision of the good life are hardly neutral; both secular and religious frameworks express fundamental convictions about meaning and value in life. This would seem to be the intent of the *Seeger* and *Welsh* decisions mentioned earlier: the violation of one's conscience, one's fundamental convictions, can occur whether or not a belief in God is involved.

The significance of this point, while perhaps obvious to some readers, should not be underestimated. Many who criticize exploration of religion in public schools fail to recognize the underlying presence and influence of non-neutral, secular-ethical frameworks. As a result, students' opportunity to engage respectfully with wide ethical difference is greatly hindered, to the ultimate detriment of a healthy public square where decisions are made about how to live together.

So while my focus in this book might generally be described as the educational exploration of religiously-informed ethical frameworks, it will also necessarily include considerations of their secular counterparts. For instance, if students are considering religious perspectives on the accumulation of wealth, an understanding of Marxism would also be educationally warranted. As I have acknowledged, some might argue that philosophies such as Marxism ought themselves to be categorized as religious, or at least as comprehensive worldviews similar to religion. For my purposes, these definitional lines need not be starkly drawn. While I will claim that religion poses some particular challenges for civic deliberation—and thus merits focused analysis in chapter 6—ethical education also needs to involve frameworks that are not commonly understood as religious. The general characteristic that makes them subjects for Ethical Dialogue is their concern with central metaphysical questions that inform a robust vision of the good life, and thus will likely impact our civic lives together. Nonreligious worldviews may generally have a more limited ethical scope, but they deserve thoughtful attention when their concerns arise in ethical discourse involving more comprehensive religious frameworks.

Because of public schools' tendency to sidestep exploration of religious-ethical frameworks, my case for the importance of Ethical Dialogue in public school classrooms focuses largely on the role of religion. The first part of this chapter sketched a conception of mutual respect and ethical identity, characterizing humans as project pursuers with (inevitable) ethical frameworks. My argument, at its broadest level, is that public schools should help students learn how to engage in respectful deliberation about these frameworks through a process of mutual understanding. My more specific focus is Ethical Dialogue involving religious frameworks (and, as I just explained, their secular counterparts). In chapter 4, I will explore how public schoolteachers might help their students engage in thoughtful Ethical Dialogue, particularly as it relates to religious understanding. Before reaching this stage of educational application, however, we need to consider more closely the link between religious and ethical identity in the lives of many students.

AMERICA'S RELIGIOUS LANDSCAPE

Even if students themselves don't voice ethical perspectives informed by religious commitments, it is still vital that they learn how to engage thoughtfully with religious-ethical disagreement. Religion is a central concern in American life, public and private; it contributes mightily to the vast diversity of ethical projects in our society. The requirements of mutual respect impel us to understand these often conflicting projects, and this includes understanding their frequently religious influences.

A common misconception exists that the United States is becoming an increasingly secular society. Certainly our society has become increasingly open to diverse ethical frameworks, but America is noteworthy as a nation for its relatively high level of religiosity—defying sociologist Peter Berger's "secularization thesis" that increasingly advanced, technologized societies would become more secular (a thesis Berger himself disowned in 1998).

National surveys regularly report anywhere from 60 percent to 85 percent of Americans claiming that religion is an important part of their lives. As a recent illustration of this sentiment, recall the national uproar over an appellate court ruling that reciting the Pledge of Allegiance in public schools is unconstitutional because of the phrase "under God."[14]

Nevertheless, the U.S. religious landscape has changed noticeably in recent decades. The tremendous influence of immigration underscores the link between religious development and broader social trends. The Immigration Act of 1965 opened U.S. borders to a vast array of non-European newcomers, many of whom also brought religious faiths other than Christianity. In the eyes of researcher Diana Eck, this influx holds broad implications for our assumptions about America as a Christian nation:

> As Muslim Americans stand in the halls of Congress, Buddhist Americans ordain monks in temples flying the American flag, Hindu Americans run for local and state office, and Sikh Americans insist on their constitutional right to wear the turban and retain their uncut hair in the military, the presupposition that America is foundationally Christian is being challenged, really for the first time. There is no going back. As we say in Montana, the horses are already out of the barn. Our new religious diversity is not just an idea but a reality, built into our neighborhoods all over America. Religious pluralism is squarely and forever on the American agenda.

Even with Christians having become more vocal and politically active in the past three decades, and in spite of lingering assumptions that equate American religion with Christianity, Eck is clear in her contention: "The United States has become the most religiously diverse nation on earth."[15]

The presence of religious diversity does not necessarily mean a shift in the nation's religious center of gravity, however, which remains predominantly Christian. As Philip Jenkins argues, "When Eck envisages 'the world's most religiously diverse nation,' she is contemplating an America that, within twenty years or so, may include a non-Christian population of at most six or seven percent, a figure that includes all Jews,

Muslims, Buddhists, Hindus, Taoists, and Sikhs." Even Eck's numbers put religious minorities at less than 10 percent of the population. Regardless, she insists, percentages do not matter, because in religious concerns, free exercise is the defining principle, not majority rule.[16]

While free exercise of religion should certainly not depend upon numerical representation, Eck's broader argument about awarding recognition to various religious groups deserves some qualifications, at least in the curricular realm. In practice, not all religious perspectives can be equally addressed in schools (or any other limited forum, for that matter). Surely some acknowledgment of what faiths and religious concepts are predominantly represented in society ought to inform pedagogical decisions, else we would be faced with the prospect of dividing our curricular attention into hundreds if not thousands of different—and unavoidably superficial—topics. Eck herself makes the point that the "new religious America" generates an even stronger imperative for cross-religious understanding, implying that greater representation by these religions on U.S. soil generates greater imperative to attend to them.

Let me be absolutely clear, however, that I am not arguing for an ethical education dominated by Christian ideology. Rather, I contend that while recognizing the growing reality of religious diversity in the United States, we also need to understand the challenges of Ethical Dialogue against the social backdrop that often carries implicit assumptions about religious normativity. On the one hand, we must realize that such dialogue can hardly result in deep understanding of all religious diversity, and we would be better served by focusing primarily on major religions. On the other hand, as Nord and Haynes point out, we need to also include some exploration of "minor" religions to avoid sending the message that these faiths are not deserving of our respect and that major religions are normative. In all cases, context and pedagogical sensitivity are vital, including special attention to local community religions.[17]

Describing the current U.S. religious landscape involves a moving target, of course. The past decade, for example, has seen Muslim benedictions at both the Republican and Democratic National Conventions and the commissioning of the U.S. Navy's first Muslim chaplain. Do such events confirm that Eck's new religious America has entered the broader national consciousness? Perhaps to a degree, but then we need only look back to the 2001 presidential inauguration of George W. Bush, where the son of renowned Christian evangelist Billy Graham concluded his prayer of invocation "in the name of the Father, and of the Son, the Lord Jesus

Christ, and of the Holy Spirit." Lest this be seen as merely political-religious rhetoric, we can also note that not soon after this event, 67 percent of respondents answered affirmatively to the question "Is the U.S. a Christian nation?" Clearly, religion is not going away; furthermore, Christianity remains the dominant influence.[18]

But just as the history books and political headlines often fail to provide an accurate picture of common life, we might well be wary of relying on traditional sources of information to draw definitive conclusions about the religious texture of our nation. Statistics measuring religious adherence are notoriously unreliable.[19] In particular, surveys are ill suited for capturing the intensity of religious commitment, often a key factor when considering how people of faith will deliberate with others in the public realm. Even given the likelihood that Christianity will continue to dominate the American religious and social consciousness, it would in fact be difficult to find another land where so many faiths are flourishing, and where demonstrating respect for fellow citizens requires a vastly improved understanding of their religious identities and the ethical frameworks that emerge from them.

ETHICAL DIALOGUE AND ROOTED RELIGIOUS IDENTITY

An understanding of religious diversity is necessary if we are to account for the richness and variety of both religious and broader cultural influences in our students, and if we are to enable them to engage with questions of deep ethical import. The ways in which individuals understand their ethical and personal identities have certainly become more complex in modern times. Traditional society offered relatively fixed answers to questions of personal identity and ethical commitments, but our modern milieu, with its loosening of traditional roles and rules, has shifted the emphasis from implicit acceptance of a social role to personal construction of identity.

Even within the broad realm of American religious belief and practice, the orientation toward religious commitment and affiliation has diversified in monumental ways. Sociologist Robert Wuthnow describes this revolution as a shift from a spirituality of place (i.e., church, community) to a spirituality of (usually eclectic) seeking. Drawing on numerous research studies, opinion surveys, and in-depth interviews, Wuthnow asserts, "People have been losing faith in a metaphysic that can make them feel at home in the universe and . . . they increasingly negotiate among competing glimpses of the sacred, seeking partial knowledge and practical wisdom." Having some sort of spiritual faith is far more important than the doctrinal details or legacy of tradition. This orientation often takes on a consumerist mentality—religion as a commodity to be shopped and compared—and has been widely documented by secular media, scholars of religion, and church builders alike.[20]

To the extent that a genuine shift has occurred in spiritual-religious orientation, at least among a major sector of American society, it obviously holds significant implications for how we conceptualize and engage with the notion of religious identity, particularly in public school settings. The conception of religious believer as seeker, freely choosing from various perspectives and experiences, playing the role of spiritual consumer, has fed an assumption that religious identity is a kind of optional garment: often useful, handily accessorized, and readily changed to suit one's personal tastes.

But this hardly describes all religious commitment, of course. For many adherents, religion is inextricably linked with one's very self, and the roots extend deep within a community of belief and practice. One is raised within such a community, and one's ethical framework and interpretive horizon are largely dependent upon this pervasive and comprehensive way of life. While not (necessarily) a servile follower, the adherent is nonetheless deeply rooted in a religious identity.

A clear tension exists here between the conceptions of seeker and rooted adherent. My intention in the remainder of this chapter is not to resolve this tension but to suggest that it contributes to the challenge of Ethical Dialogue between those with a seeker mentality and those with a rooted, religious identity (both seeker and rooted orientations could also include nonreligious, secular individuals). As I asserted in chapter 2, much ethical education curricula and pedagogy in public schools is unhelpfully tilted toward a seeker mentality.

It is this devaluing of rooted religious identity, I believe, that provokes many conservative religious families to turn elsewhere for their children's education. In this sense, contemporary public schools risk the same error that Charles Glenn accuses the common school reformers of the nineteenth century of making: "not their generous vision—universal education that would reach the heart as well as the head of every future citizen—but their ungenerosity toward the stubborn particularities of loyalty and conviction, the 'mediating structures' and world views, by which people actually live." As apparent evidence of this dissatisfaction, the U.S. Department of Education measured a 3.4 percent increase in enrollment at evangelical Christian schools during the 1990s; even more significantly, federal data revealed a 29 percent increase in homeschooling between 1999 and 2003. While certainly public schools should not respond to such reports by returning to the singular, oppressive ethical model I described in chapter 2, we also should not underestimate the importance of keeping as many students and citizens as possible involved in ethical conversations where a diversity of perspectives can be recognized and understood.[21]

Another way in which rooted religious identity seems to be overlooked in public schools is in multicultural education, which often includes the experiences of immigrants to the United States, presently and historically. But the strong connection between immigrants' ethnic and religious identity often goes unexplored in multicultural curricula. A growing research literature emphasizes religion as a mediator of immigrant identities, observing that religious identity often becomes even more important to new immigrants as they navigate a process of assimilation while still seeking to preserve self-identity. In addition, religion often helps maintain links to traditional culture for second-generation immigrants. Given these dynamics, the lack of attention to religion in multicultural curricula is deeply unfortunate, and ultimately misleading to students seeking a better understanding of social and ethical diversity.[22]

This strong relationship between religion and identity is not limited to immigrants, of course. For many adherents, their religion is inextricably linked with their identity. An approach to Ethical Dialogue that is sufficiently (and respectfully) inclusive must acknowledge not only this reality, but also the myriad ways that religious adherence informs that identity. For some, their ethical framework is constructed largely independently of their religious commitments; for others, doctrinal creeds shape their response to ethical concerns; for still others, a community of tradition and religious observance dictates their orientation to the good life.

A cogent explanation of this latter dynamic is offered by theologian Roberto Goizueta, who describes a "theology of accompaniment" for U.S. Hispanic Catholics. He observes, "My identity is given me by my parents, relatives, friends, and many other relationships and communities; there is no 'I' without all these others. I am a particular, concrete, and unique embodiment of all those relationships; when someone encounters me, they also encounter my parents, relatives, friends, community, my people, as well as the God who created me and the earth which nourishes me." It makes no sense for such a believer to consider his faith apart from his community; both deeply influence his sense of identity and ethical framework. Goizueta contrasts this perspective with what he describes as a typical Anglo-American orientation, which understands relationship with God as an individual enterprise and communal participation as secondary to religious belief.[23] The potential superiority of one orientation over the other is not my concern here; what matters for Ethical Dialogue is that students recognize such distinctions when considering how ethical frameworks are constructed. When an ethical perspective is forwarded that emerges from a "theology of accompaniment," for example, respect requires that we understand its inherent links with a broader set of relationships that extend well beyond religious doctrine.

The relationship between various religious perspectives and personal identity can generate an entirely different challenge for Ethical Dialogue as well. The theory of mutual respect that I have advocated depends on an implicit assumption about the worth of the self: our value resides in our particularity, in the narrative structure of our project pursuit. While my foundational claim stops well short of extremist arguments that privilege autonomy above all other goods, it will likely encounter resistance from ethical frameworks that do not recognize the value of the self, or even the notion of the self at all. Among major religions, this concern is perhaps most salient regarding Buddhism. While some versions do affirm the existence of a self, there is clearly an orientation in much Buddhist thought that would find the idea of a personal narrative informing an ethical framework to be nonsensical.[24] It seems unavoidable that denial of, or at least agnosticism concerning, the very existence of the self leads to a similar attitude about the *value* of the self.

Here we need to recognize an important distinction. Many religions (and other ethical frameworks) that do not accept the entire theoretical justification I have offered for Ethical Dialogue can still be involved in such discourse, not only as subjects of consideration but also by adherents of that religion. For example, students can seek to understand the tradition of Buddhist thought that is agnostic about matters of the self, and deliberate thoughtfully about how such an ethical framework is to be respectfully accommodated in society. The philosophical rationale of Ethical Dialogue does not preclude an ethics of "no self" from being understood and respected.[25]

Ethical Dialogue must not only contend with the ways in which different religions conceive of identity, of course, but also the models of identity development constructed by modern *secular* society. These secular conceptions typically view identity as "a continuous activity of construction and deconstruction, of developing, maintaining, and evaluating personal commitments to values, persons, and practices."[26] On one level, this seems inevitably true of any process of identity formation; our social environment generates ongoing influence in our lives. But the degree to which we see ourselves as actively constructing and deconstructing meaning through evaluation of personal commitments varies widely depending upon our broader ethical framework. Some religious faiths will resist any attempts to make revision of identity the desired norm.

Nevertheless, because public schools are generally comprised of individuals with a diversity of ethical frameworks, they will have an almost inevitable impact on ethical identity, whether this is informed by religious sources or not. Public education presents students with more ethical alternatives than most would encounter outside their schools, potentially complicating their own ethical framework. Some rooted adherents will find this process not only challenging but deeply threatening. As teachers seek to foster Ethical Dialogue in their classrooms, they must be sensitive to this issue. As I argue in the chapters that follow, this sensitivity must include an understanding that is not sufficiently expressed in much developmental education literature: revision of one's ethical framework is not an inherent good. The rooted adherent, whose ethical sources often rely on tradition and community beyond her own individuality, must have these commitments respected as well. While a certain willingness to engage with ethical diversity is essential for true dialogue, this need not presume that ethical revision should always emerge from it. In many cases, the wiser outcome may well be to adhere to one's prior ethical framework.

Throughout this book, I present the idea of the "ethical" as encompassing far more than (what is often referred to as) the moral realm, meaning morality as obligation and exclusively concerned with matters of right and wrong. This distinction is crucially important when considering the notion of religious identity; for many religious adherents, isolating moral obligation from broader ethical issues is a largely incoherent exercise. Questions of moral obligation often make sense only within a larger vision of the good life. When this broader ethical conception includes religious influences, then morality and religion are often deeply intertwined.

In contrast, much current moral education theory and curricula argue that since many basic moral concerns appear widely shared by humans, moral education can proceed independently from religious considerations.[27] But this underestimates the extent to which religious belief can influence broader concepts of human flourishing, which in turn affect one's judgments of others' interests. As Eamonn Callan points out, "If I had faith, my relationship to God would not just be added to my existing scheme of values, like a new interest in stamp-collecting, say, which governs choice only within a segment of life I assign to the interest. The life of faith is driven by devotion to God, which means that embracing it would oblige me to think altogether differently about what matters in my life and the lives of others."[28]

While many religious adherents rely on their personal moral judgment as a means of reflection and validation of their religiously-shaped ethical framework, their lives and moral actions are nonetheless shaped directly by the force of those religious commitments. A rational desire to have one's faith resonate with one's moral intuitions does not necessarily mean that the former is dictated by the latter. And while ethical deliberation in civic society involves a search for common ground, cultivating this ground does not depend on the wholesale exclusion of religious perspectives and how they inform moral beliefs. In fact, such exclusion will hinder educational efforts to engage students with moral complexities as they play out in their lives and the society in which they live.

Ethical Dialogue involves an acknowledgment of the complex relationship between religion, ethics, and obligations and how this reality helps shape our society and the lives of many in it. In a world marked by great diversity of ethical projects, mutual respect requires that we understand how and why we disagree. Developing the capacity for such understanding requires an intentional educational focus; as Benjamin Barber contends, "We may be natural consumers and born narcissists, but citizens have to be made."[29] The next three chapters offer an educational vision for the development of such citizens, beginning with an emphasis on empathic understanding of ethical difference and progressing to a capacity for respectful political deliberation concerning those differences.

4

Imaginative Engagement
with Ethical Difference

As chapter 1 explained, the central question of this project is "How can we learn to talk and make decisions about living together in the face of our divergent convictions about the best ways to live?" Chapter 3 began with the assertion that mutual respect must serve as a foundation for any good society and argued that this respect requires understanding what is of central importance in the lives of others, their "ethical frameworks." In an ethically diverse society such as ours, these frameworks will often conflict. Given this inevitability, we must learn to deliberate thoughtfully about many of these disagreements, at least as they affect our lives together. This is the goal of Ethical Dialogue, and public schools are a crucial setting for such learning to occur.

The practice of Ethical Dialogue, as I describe it in the remainder of this book, involves two basic elements: imaginative engagement and civic deliberation. The former strives for the sort of mutual understanding I advocated in chapter 3; the latter involves using this understanding to help us make decisions about how we are to live together in society.[1] Making such decisions will require us to evaluate conflicting ethical frameworks and generate compromises that allow us to live together in reasonable disagreement. Ethical Dialogue, then, is a multifaceted conversation: respectful engagement with different ethical frameworks needs to include critical evaluation (lest it be empty patronizing), but this evaluation must first rest on an ongoing effort toward imaginative understanding of those diverse frameworks.

The purpose of this chapter is to explain this process of imaginative engagement as the vital groundwork of Ethical Dialogue. While classroom efforts toward imaginative engagement involve considerable challenge, I want to emphasize that this is not an esoteric endeavor intended only for budding young philosophers. The necessary mix of cognitive and affective elements requires both pedagogical humility and care, but in this respect is no different than broader efforts toward multicultural education. Many public schools have found good reason to make the latter a significant curricular emphasis, and Ethical Dialogue—as a vital contribution to thoughtful citizenship—deserves similar commitment.

A DEEPER SENSE OF APPRECIATION

Ethical reflection requires, at its core, the ability to imagine beyond ourselves. The type of imagination required here in fact embodies what a true liberal education should be about, enabling students to engage with the rich diversity of human development and understanding of the world. In particular, imaginative engagement is a crucial element of multicultural education in its intent to provide an understanding and appreciation of cultural diversity. It should go without saying—but clearly needs to be said in the context of public education—that a major contributor to this diversity is religion, and that religious sources have played a pivotal role in human development *writ* large.

There is general consensus (at least in intention) that religion has a place in the school curriculum, at least as it informs our understanding of history and past cultures. But if we ask the question "Is a curriculum which explores and compares the religious beliefs of ancient Aztecs, Mayas, and Babylonians any different from one that does so with Islam, Christianity, and Judaism?" then perhaps the realization emerges that the latter religions are more than static historical markers. Rather, they are vibrant, deeply influential ethical and cultural forces in our society, and any education claiming the label "liberal" or "multicultural" must engage imaginatively with them and other living religions.

Thoughtful evaluation of foreign ethical frameworks, religious or otherwise, requires an empathic understanding of those frameworks. "To understand people," asserts Warren Nord, "we must hear what they say and see what they do in the context of their beliefs about the world, their philosophical assumptions, their reasoning, their motives. To understand a religion is to be able to look out on the world and on human experience and see and feel it from the viewpoint of the categories of that religion."[2] In many cases, this involves fostering an appreciation for *why* something apparently insignificant (from the outside) is of great or even sacred importance to insiders. While this doesn't necessarily mean that we will agree with this different perspective, it provides us the opportunity to gain insight into what gives meaning to the lives of others and to demonstrate respect for them as equal members of the polity.

Clearly more is involved here than just propositional knowledge about other ways of life, more than lists of doctrines or characteristics. Stephen Darwall's notion of "appreciation" offers a useful perspective on the goal of imaginative engagement. When I encounter a different ethical framework, I may value or appreciate the virtue of learning more about it. I may even appreciate the virtue of tolerating it in the lives of others. Neither of these is sufficient, though, for imaginative engagement. My appreciation must also extend to the particularity of the other ethical framework, toward what is valued in the framework itself. As students explore the way a particular religion envisions strict gender roles, for instance, they should strive to understand and appreciate what value those boundaries hold in that religion and its community of adherents. For example, students must strive to temporarily put aside, as much as possible, any personal convictions that gender equality requires equal opportunity, and consider the possible value of more predetermined social roles. The goal here is not to change students' beliefs but to widen their appreciation for ways of life different than their own. Such imaginative engagement is, to borrow Deborah Kerdeman's phrase, "a negotiation between familiarity and strangeness."[3]

One drawback of Darwall's terminology, however, is that "appreciation" is commonly associated with approval or at least acceptance. Does this mean that imaginative engagement requires students to find value in all ethical frameworks they encounter? Certainly not. An effort to appreciate the value in a different ethical framework does not necessitate a slide into relativism or subjectivism. Even when we recognize that other ethical goods may exist beyond our own framework, this is a long way from conceding that all frameworks are equally valid. Ethical diversity—any diversity, for that matter—is not a good unto itself, nor can all frameworks be valued in a society whose foundation rests on the principle of respect for others. Still, imaginative engagement fosters room for students to recognize ethical good beyond the familiarity of their own frameworks.

We must avoid mindless subjectivism but also guard against a lack of interpretive goodwill in seeking to understand the perspectives of others. We should avoid concluding prematurely that ethical frameworks are incommensurable; this often reveals a failure of imagination in navigating difference rather than an insurmountable epistemological roadblock.

Not only does imaginative engagement not require a subjectivist stance, it also should not privilege the idea of an ethical framework undergoing constant revision. Appreciating ethical diversity does not entail students revising their own frameworks at every turn. As I discuss more fully in chapter 6, the value of adherence (to ethical tradition, for example) is frequently overlooked in our modern society. Recognizing the value of ethical *commitment* is an equally important lesson for students. Students should be encouraged to recognize and appreciate their own anchored perspectives, while at the same time valuing the good in other ethical frameworks where they find it. I might appreciate the stability and close community of an insular culture with predetermined social roles, for instance, while still holding fast to an ethic of social mobility and unlimited equality of opportunity.

One additional, crucial observation about appreciation is necessary. In my discussion of civic deliberation in chapter 5, I begin with the claim that reasonable people will inevitably disagree about the good life. The goal of imaginative engagement is to lay the groundwork that enables students to recognize the reasonableness of differing points of view. Accepting this notion of reasonable disagreement does not, however, necessarily entail a belief in ethical pluralism—the conviction that these other perspectives are correct, that there are multiple sources of ethical value. There is room in Ethical Dialogue for both ethical pluralists and ethical monists. Imaginative engagement is aimed at appreciating the reasonableness of divergent ethical frameworks, not necessarily agreement with those beliefs.

The goals here are to gain a deeper understanding of others' ethical perspectives and to clarify one's own views, reflecting on them in light of differing perspectives. For example, students might engage in a discussion of school holidays, with some religious/cultural minorities expressing their dissatisfaction with public schools' observance of Christmas (for some schools, this would include various ceremonies or pageants, but for all of them, at least a week of vacation). This would serve as an opportunity for such minorities to share about their own primary holidays, and for students in the (loosely defined) Christian majority to engage imaginatively with such questions as "How might I feel about the school calendar if I celebrated these other holidays instead?" Students would be encouraged to reflect on the significance of Christmas as both a religious and secular event, considering it from their own perspective of observance or nonobservance as well as striving to understand how others might agree or disagree with them. Depending on the developmental level of the students, the discussion might extend into broader social questions of majority/minority cultures and their recognition and representation in the public square.

In addition, students who celebrate Christmas and support continued school observance would be invited to share their perspectives but then asked to reflect on how someone else might critique their beliefs. They would be encouraged to consider the intended religious neutrality of schools that nevertheless surround this holiday with a week or more of school vacation, while generally providing no break for many other groups' holidays, religious or otherwise. Conversely, non-Christians would be asked to consider how their arguments might fare if proponents of "Christmas break" conceive of the holiday as primarily secular, akin to the government's observance of Thanksgiving and Memorial Day.

Encouraging students to ask these questions serves at least three functions. First, in culturally homogeneous environments, critiques of the dominant majority will be less apparent, and citizens need to consider differing viewpoints even when those voices are not present themselves. It is important to stress, however, that teachers (and societies) need to make every effort to provide a forum for first-person ethical expressions; in strongly homogeneous schools, this might include guest speakers, literature, and multimedia. Nevertheless, there may be times when this is not possible, such as consideration of those who literally cannot speak for themselves, including the very young and the physically/mentally incapacitated.

Second, encouraging students to consider how others might view their own beliefs is a crucial step in fostering genuine dialogue. If I cannot even conceive of objections to my ethical framework, the possibility of learning from those who disagree seems remote if not impossible. It is not enough to know that others disagree with me; I need to have some appreciation for why their framework cannot accommodate mine.

A third benefit of this process not specifically related to Ethical Dialogue, but worth noting nonetheless, is the educational value—in terms of developing critical thinking—of taking a different position on an issue and arguing it with evidence and insight. Skilled teachers know the value of this technique whenever students believe an issue to be undeniably one-sided, when in fact it contains unrecognized complexity. Having to make the best case possible for a position they reject may also encourage the habit of "charitable interpretation"—taking an opposing perspective at its best, rather than immediately seeking to identify its weaknesses.

OUR CAPACITY FOR EMPATHIC UNDERSTANDING

The idea of imaginative engagement and, in particular, empathic understanding will likely prompt objections from some that we can never really understand the perspectives of others from the inside, and it is dangerous to assume that we can. While there is much validity to this concern, we should avoid the opposite extreme as well. As Clifford Geertz observes, "The truth of the doctrine of cultural . . . relativism is that we can never apprehend another people's or another period's imagination neatly, as though it were our own. The falsity of it is that we can therefore never genuinely apprehend it at all." We can certainly be more or less understanding of a foreign ethical framework, and while there will undoubtedly be contexts in which our comprehension is limited, this hardly justifies abdicating our obligation to try.[4]

Other detractors may question the degree to which empathic engagement is possible in younger children. Developmental psychology has generated a substantial research literature on empathy and provides some useful insight into this question. While Piagetian constructs assert that it is not until about age seven that children can both recognize that others have their own perspective and adopt the viewpoint of another, other researchers have suggested that it may happen earlier, perhaps as young as age three. One survey of current research on ethical education concludes that the major advances in our capacity to understand others' points of view occur between ages four and twelve—accordingly, elementary and middle schools play a crucial role in the nurturing of this capacity. While psychological research offers differing opinions as to the particular ages at which developmental transitions occur involving empathy and perspective taking, an experienced teacher realizes that her students are almost inevitably at different developmental stages anyway. Thus what seems most important is this recognition on the teacher's part that her students—particularly prior to adolescence—vary in their capacity for empathic understanding, and the routes to imaginative engagement will need to be as multimodal as any other element in her curriculum.[5]

Empathic understanding of religion by nonadherents would seem to be an especially daunting endeavor, particularly to the extent that we accept Augustine's oft-cited *credo ut intelligiam*—"we must believe in order to understand." The idea here is that outsiders cannot understand the perspectives of insiders, and insiders cannot communicate their beliefs intelligibly. But this position is too extreme; as Roberto Goizueta points out, "I cannot claim that my cultural perspective is particular and unique to me unless and until I have some knowledge of other cultural perspectives—which knowledge would already imply the possibility of self-transcendence."[6] At least some degree of translation and comprehension across ethical frameworks is available to us.

At the same time, we should not underestimate the distance between differing ethical perspectives. Uma Narayan describes the notion of "epistemic privilege" that should be accorded insiders, particularly those whose experiences are marked by substantial oppression. Outsiders will have difficulty appreciating the myriad ways in which oppression impacts the lives of its victims. This doesn't mean, however, that outsiders can't come to understand insider experiences, nor that epistemic privilege is infallible. What is called for, asserts Narayan, are the twin virtues of methodological humility (wherein I acknowledge that I may be missing something) and methodological caution (wherein I take great care in translation to reduce the chance I will misinterpret). I acknowledge the reality of my status as outsider while resisting stereotyping as well as the notion that other perspectives are completely closed to my comprehension.[7]

While we should certainly be cognizant of insider experience and understanding when striving for imaginative engagement, we should also resist seeing that status of insider as a monolithic category. Not only are moral understandings different across cultures, they are often different within cultures as well. We often neglect this diversity due to our tendency to focus on public symbols (e.g., the pope and his pronouncements) or be satisfied with understanding the dominant perspective within a culture (e.g., Islam's demand for theocracy). Nor should we assume that because our outsider understanding can never be complete that we should refrain from evaluating the ethical perspectives of others, or even that we cannot. To assume this would be to make the nonsensical claim that insiders' ethical beliefs cannot be mistaken. Critical listening and response are in fact signs of respect, as Walter Parker argues; otherwise we patronize the insider by refusing to engage in criticism and challenge—she becomes, in effect, merely a storyteller.[8]

This diversity of ethical perspectives even within a particular cultural or religious tradition points to the value of drawing from a variety of sources. The best informants, John Stuart Mill asserts, are those who hold those particular beliefs themselves. As I mentioned previously, teachers (and societies) need to make every effort to provide a forum for first-person ethical expressions. One obvious—and important—source is students themselves. Such an approach resonates strongly with the broader principles of multicultural education, which strive to offer a fuller representation and exploration of cultural diversity, particularly as it reflects the experiences and heritages of students. Providing opportunity for students to connect personal experience with broader ethical issues will likely result in some students insisting that their own experience is a privileged way of knowing, but as bell hooks points out, when teachers affirm the importance of personal experience, students may feel less need to assert its primacy over and against all other sources of understanding. She cites Henry Giroux's admonition to teachers: "You can't deny that students have experiences and you can't deny that these experiences are relevant to the learning process even though you might say these experiences are limited, raw, unfruitful or whatever. Students have memories, families, religions, feelings, languages and cultures that give them a distinctive voice. We can critically engage that experience and we can move beyond it. But we can't deny it." Our public schools, however, frequently deny or ignore these textures of students' lives, thereby denying students the crucial learning opportunity to connect their necessarily limited experiences to broader ethical ideas and social concerns.[9]

The educational value of student experience as a route to imaginative engagement speaks to the benefits of an ethically diverse classroom, as Vivian Paley observes in her reflections on multicultural education: "We are constantly called upon to explain our differences to each other. . . . *To look for ways to explain who we are:* this would seem to be a fundamental requirement for us all in a classroom." Paley asserts that even kindergartners can provide valuable insight into their own cultures, but acknowledges that there are times that adults need to assist with the expression and translation. Certainly as students grow older, they gain capacity to effectively share their ethical beliefs, but even here caution is required. Students should have the opportunity to share their perspectives, but we should also recognize that they are often not going to be the most sophisticated representatives of a given ethical framework.[10]

Student expression of ethical beliefs holds additional challenges as well. When discussing the idea of imaginative engagement during a graduate seminar, one of my students grew increasingly enthusiastic about how rich and affirming such an experience could be for students; they should, she asserted, "be able to bring everything, all of their intensity about their beliefs" into the classroom. At this point, another seminar participant, who had taught for years in the public schools, balked: "As a teacher, that feels very dangerous for me. I want my kids engaged, sure, but there have to be some limits!" The appropriate limits on such intensity will vary according to classroom context, of course. At the same time, however, I doubt many good teachers would want their classrooms to be places where feelings and expressions of deep personal commitment are largely discouraged.

While the disagreement in my graduate seminar focused primarily on protecting other students in the class, we should also keep in mind that great care should be afforded those who actually choose to share ethical convictions. While there is certainly educational benefit in sharing one's deeply held views in an atmosphere of trust and caring, challenges remain. Even when a safe and supportive classroom environment is available, students may (understandably) not be sufficiently sensitive to the personal significance of values, traditions, and experiences that their peers describe. Unless the listeners actually share those experiences "from the inside," the dangers of misinterpretation and even trivialization are significant.[11] This concern is most prevalent, however, in situations of required, formalized classroom sharing; there are certainly other, less risky means by which students can express their personal perspectives. One useful approach might be to ask students to write a confidential critique of the way their religion is being presented (via classroom texts, etc.)—this allows them to express their own perspective while also giving the teacher some potentially valuable feedback on her curricular design.

Pedagogical caution is clearly a prime consideration in imaginative engagement. To drive this point home, Robert Nash offers five rules for engaging in pluralistic ethical dialogue; the final three all end with the same admonition: "Proceed with utmost caution at all times."[12] But this should not dissuade teachers from cultivating an atmosphere in which first-person insight is valued and encouraged. There will be many times, however, when either students are uncomfortable sharing their perspectives, or the ethical frameworks under consideration are not shared by members of the classroom. Even when students do contribute, teachers should also make liberal use of literature, multimedia, primary and secondary texts, guest speakers, and other relevant sources. Inviting guest speakers, of course, requires special due diligence on the teacher's part to ensure that speakers do not act as proselytizers or definitive spokespeople for a particular tradition. All of these resources have the potential to contribute to both cognitive and affective understanding, a process I call "stirring the ethical imagination."

STIRRING THE ETHICAL IMAGINATION

If student understanding is to extend beyond a merely informational level about ethical difference to the kind of substantive appreciation described earlier, it must include a broader, affective component. Imaginative engagement is more than simply an intellectual exercise, just as empathy involves an emotional recognition of another perspective. This cognition-plus-affect approach seems particularly important in the context of religion, where imaginative engagement helps us move beyond a purely doctrinal understanding that, while predominant in Abrahamic faiths, is less important in other religions. As I explained in chapter 3, religion frequently includes rich facets of tradition, community, and ritual—it provides a way of *being in the world* that generally includes propositional beliefs, but whose significance for adherents extends well beyond this.

Three common pedagogical techniques for encouraging a fuller imaginative understanding are role-plays, field experiences, and art and stories. As with most curricular approaches, their success lies in *how* they are used. In the pursuit of imaginative engagement, it seem equally crucial that teachers understand the *limitations* of various approaches. While the imagination can be a powerful means of bridging gaps of understanding, we run the risk—especially with terrain as potentially hazardous as religion—of assuming too much. We need not overreach to gain an importantly useful appreciation of ethical diversity.

Role-Plays

"From the beginning," the class handout read, "you and your classmates will become Muslims." Like most public schools in America, Excelsior was attempting to address state standards. Over the course of several weeks in 2002, seventh-grade students in this Oakland area middle school engaged in role-plays aimed at furthering their understanding of Islam.

Activities included choosing Islamic names for themselves, playing a board game that simulated a pilgrimage to Mecca, and memorizing portions of Islamic proverbs and prayers to recite for their teacher. Students also had the option to dress up in Islamic robes for extra credit. Parents of some students filed suit, claiming violation of First Amendment prohibitions on the teaching of religion in public school. The classroom teacher countered that she had made it clear throughout the unit that such activities were prefaced with "let's pretend"; in addition, she stated that her intent was never to proselytize or indoctrinate students.[13]

One frequently abused technique in many classrooms is that of role-playing. This commonly results in the oversimplification of complex ethical issues and is particularly problematic in the exploration of religion. Too often these attempts share flaws similar to (though perhaps not as obvious as) this Oakland middle-school curriculum unit. In light of the myriad social variables and influences that cannot possibly be simulated, oversimplification becomes the almost inevitable outcome. Efforts to "become Muslims" for a ninety-minute class period, for instance, are likely to be offensive to both non-Muslims (who may balk at enacting religious practices) and Muslims (who see their faith being trivialized through playacting).

Role-playing has educational value, I believe, only in conveying very specific experiences and perspectives to the actors and audience. Rather than expecting that students will be able to become Muslims in any substantive sense, an appropriate role-play might involve a student requesting special school accommodations (e.g., being excused from class at specific times for prayer) and meeting with ignorance and resistance from administrators. The goal would be to gain an empathic understanding of some of the challenges in living out a minority religion in the dominant Protestant-secular culture, but teachers should be alert not to convey the message "Now you've experienced what it's like to be a Muslim." Clearly the range of epistemic privilege that Narayan describes earlier is far greater and deeper than any simulation can convey.

In addition, teachers must be cognizant of the developmental capacities of their students; while some older high school students might benefit from a role-play involving religiously arranged marriages, for example, it seems unlikely that younger students would appreciate its complexity (emotional and otherwise). In sum, if role-playing is used by teachers, it should be done so with extreme care and with a very specific and limited outcome in mind.

Field Experiences

A more promising experiential approach to imaginative engagement is the field experience. Physically entering an unfamiliar cultural community can provide rich insight into the lives and perspectives of others. The principle of "more is better" would seem to be largely in effect here: the longer participants can spend in the cultural setting and relinquish their own comfortable patterns, the better. So the ideal end of the continuum would be some sort of semester or year-long cultural immersion in an unfamiliar setting; research confirms the value of such extended experiential learning.[14] Spend time listening to a student who has just returned from a semester abroad: the tales of "culture shock"—both leaving and returning to her home—suggest the power of such an immersion.

When considering options for the classroom curriculum, however, an extended immersion experience is rarely feasible. This is where the other end of the field experience continuum carries worrisome miseducative possibilities. A one-day field trip by suburban students to an inner-city school, for example, can reinforce stereotypes rather than provide the opportunity to see beyond them. Unless students have the opportunity to talk with and learn from their urban counterparts, perhaps engage in a mutual endeavor, the opportunity to gain a better sense of the urban students' reality will likely be lost.

The same holds true for exploration of ethical diversity. A visit to a local mosque or synagogue may provide some helpful images and information but miss out on much more, if the experience does not include opportunities to interact with adherents in ways that communicate the religion's vibrancy and profound influence on its community. Experiences in which students remain passive and detached observers of a setting rarely provide the engagement necessary for substantive appreciation of ethical diversity.

Art and Stories

Another entrée to such appreciation is through the arts, and in particular the power of stories, which can provide eloquent expression to the challenge of moral indeterminacy and the complexity of ethical pluralism. The use of "texts" such as stories, poems, music, plays, films, paintings, and other visual arts can stir the ethical imagination in several ways. One benefit is that they can offer students a window into otherwise unavailable worlds and experiences. The study of historical figures and various doctrines contributes important background, of course, but the complex texture that an artistic rendering provides of a character or setting can foster a degree of insight and appreciation that cognitive understanding alone cannot.

Great care needs to be taken in selecting such resources, of course, but they can often provide rich context and—when developmentally appropriate—a range of ethical ambiguity that approximates real life more closely than a list of religious doctrines and principles can convey. In addition, they can help illuminate the challenges of living as a religious minority in a culture that has little understanding or appreciation of one's rich heritage and beliefs. The story of Ganesh in Malcolm Bosse's *Ordinary Magic*, for example, tells of his displacement as a boy from his native India to the American Midwest; looking through his eyes, young readers may begin to appreciate the value of empathy and understanding ethical difference.

One challenge with such texts—particularly involving highly unfamiliar settings—is getting students fully engaged even while they remain in their familiar physical environment. Appreciating the power and poignancy of Holocaust survivor Sonia Weitz's poetry or the image of Jews reciting the Kaddish at the close of *Schindler's List* can be difficult for students when the pep band is practicing outside.

Nevertheless, the very nature of the arts themselves, how they beckon to the observer to journey to someplace new and often unfamiliar, helps bridge gaps of understanding that mere cognition cannot. "Knowing 'about,'" Maxine Greene reminds us, "is entirely different from constituting a fictive world imaginatively and entering it perceptually, affectively, and cognitively."[15] At times, perhaps the greatest contribution of the arts is sparking emotional engagement in ways that a rational argument simply cannot do. This multilayered knowing is essential for students and citizens to understand others with dramatically different experiences and perspectives, to appreciate what they value and why. This is the type of understanding we need in order to live together with respect.

The power of story is not limited to artistic fiction, of course. Since the "ethical" encompasses not only questions of moral obligation (what is it good to do?) but also broader existential concerns (who is it good to be?), the consideration of the lives of so-called "moral exemplars" holds promise as well. This approach has been enjoying something of a recent revival, at least in terms of empirical research and curricular development.

Claims for the value of ethical exemplars are at least as old as Aristotle and resonate with some versions of modern character development. But the most promising models avoid the sanitized, oversimplified images of much character education. "Simply plastering the classroom walls with virtue labels will do little, if anything, to engender good moral character; rather, children need to appreciate the complexities and perhaps even the maladaptive aspects of many virtues such as honesty and care, and to struggle daily with how to exemplify these virtues," asserts psychologist Lawrence Walker. "It is important that lives in all their fullness are examined, not just heroes' statements or actions, but rather the complexity of their personalities, the formative aspects of their experiences, and their weaknesses and struggles." The appropriateness of this textured, "warts and all" approach obviously depends on the developmental level of students, but one can imagine, for example, high school students gaining an even greater appreciation for the personal risks Oskar Schindler took during the Holocaust on behalf of Jews when viewed in light of his propensity for self-advancement and financial gain.[16]

Finally, I should point out here that while the arts are a particularly potent avenue for imaginative engagement, this should in no way imply that Ethical Dialogue belongs primarily in the humanities. The discussion of genetic research from my English class, for instance, would be at least as appropriate in a biology class. The best science classes will integrate the arts into their curriculum; in the same way, my *Brave New World* class discussion would have undoubtedly been better served by exposure to at least some basic science on genetic research.

Combining Head and Heart

I have used the term *imaginative* in this chapter to emphasize that efforts to understand unfamiliar ethical perspectives must be more than cognitive-analytical exercises of factual comprehension and dispassionate comparison. In this sense it disputes vulgar Kantian interpretations that conceive of rationality apart from emotions and metaphor. But while affective insight is necessary for ethical appreciation, it is rarely sufficient; analytical understanding should not be left behind. An ethical imagination whose understanding is based solely on the arts will face an excess of meaning and an indeterminacy that hinders ethical decision.[17] Students will not be able to appreciate the richness and complexity of many ethical frameworks, and likely not be able to gain any empathic insight, if they do not have the opportunity to construct a groundwork of factual-analytical understanding as well. This might include historical and cultural information, creedal beliefs and their sources, apologetic responses to criticism, and diversity of interpretation within that framework. The type and depth of knowledge will obviously differ according to grade/developmental level, but the principle still holds.

Consider a simple curricular example of combining head and heart. At many grade levels throughout the United States, students study the "westward expansion" of white settlers across North America. A curriculum striving for greater imaginative engagement would need to include investigation of American Indian cultures, histories, and ethical frameworks. Sacred "origin stories" from various tribes would reveal a belief in tribal rights and connections to land and a narrative portraying a natural order ultimately disrupted by the arrival of whites. We might foresee a sixth-grade social studies class discussion eventually focusing on current land claims by various tribes. The teacher could draw students' attention to the Sioux tribe's ongoing refusal to accept monetary damages for the U.S. government's violation of an 1870 land treaty granting the Black Hills in South Dakota to the tribe. For a people wrestling with tremendous poverty, a $570 million settlement offer might initially seem to students to be the best option. But if students—through a growing understanding of Sioux religious beliefs that view their land as sacred—are able to recognize the central, sustaining role that religion plays in the Sioux culture, and thus see the choice as one between material and spiritual sustenance, they gain a far richer understanding of both the culture and the political controversy. A discussion of the land's role in sacred ritual might involve suggesting a parallel with church or temple rituals with which many students are likely familiar. Asking those students whether they would sell their place of worship as a means of improving their standard of living might foster a new level of engagement with the issue.

A commitment to developing students' cognitive understanding of religion is particularly lacking in public schools. One comprehensive review of how national and state social studies standards address religion points to an "almost total lack of coverage" of the past millennium that encourages "stereotyped, essentialist views of these cultures" and an assumption that "religion has faded as an influence in Western culture and remains a troublesome relic in less advanced parts of the world." Other studies have pointed to the inattention to religion in textbooks and teachers' lack of confidence in their ability to address even the standards on religion that currently exist.[18] Delving into the complexities of religion and other ethical frameworks, of course, requires time and resources; such an approach clearly has implications for the ongoing debate between depth and breadth of study. "A mile wide and an inch deep," often the norm in schools where voluminous lists of content standards dog a teacher's every step, cannot foster the level of understanding necessary for imaginative engagement.

The curricular news isn't all bad, however. The burgeoning educational use of the Internet and other technologies has provided impressive access to an array of information on religion. Extensive scholarly research such as Harvard University's Pluralism Project has been transferred onto CD and is widely available, providing access to primary source documents and engaging multimedia formats. The Internet has become a rich trove of information as well, but one that requires careful cross-checking to ascertain accuracy. But what is crucial to recognize here is that access to such materials is hardly sufficient, as chapter 7 will argue. Religion as a curricular side note, absent any support in professional development, is hardly better than ignoring it altogether—perhaps even worse, given its potential misuse. This seems especially true when the topic is as complex and sensitive as religion; most teachers will quite understandably avoid delving into these topics, particularly as they surround ethical issues, if they are neither required to do so nor supported in their efforts.

IMAGINATIVE ENGAGEMENT: THE GROUNDWORK OF DELIBERATION

If we think of civic deliberation—wherein we decide how to live together in society—as a sort of societal construction project, then imaginative engagement serves as the underlying foundation. Informed, appreciative understanding of other ethical perspectives enables our decisions to involve more than uninformed tolerance or strategic bargaining. Granted, we still need procedural safeguards to protect our interests: decisions that invoke the power of the state (sometimes involving coercion of dissenters) are a necessary component of civic life, and the procedures used to reach those decisions should be guided by constitutional principles that protect the rights of individuals. Most of us would prefer laws, not just dependence on others' empathy and goodwill, to preserve our vital interests.

But this reliance on procedural safeguards for decision making, while obviously crucial in an ethically diverse society, often obscures the importance of a civic virtue committed to real understanding of other ethical perspectives on their own terms.

The vital link between imaginative engagement and civic deliberation becomes clearer when we recognize that, in many cases, students will probably not have the exposure or insight necessary for immediate, informed deliberation about civic disagreements. Plenty of teenagers—not to mention younger students—will have never taken time to develop thoughtful positions on affirmative action, stem cell research, or many other important topics. While they may have a passing familiarity with the basic pros and cons of a given issue, it's unlikely that many students will have considered how their ethical framework and those of fellow citizens actually inform a range of positions.

Developing this type of imaginative understanding, I have claimed, involves a combination of head and heart, cognitive and affective insights. I recently observed a simple but effective example of how this might be fostered in the classroom. A public high school teacher began his lesson by asking students what they knew about their own school dress code. After sketching out its (fairly minimal) requirements, he asked students whether they were familiar with the "school uniform" strategy that some public schools had implemented in recent years, both to deemphasize socioeconomic disparities and pressures as well as to generate a sense of commonality intended to bolster school spirit. They discussed the pros and cons of such policies briefly, and then this teacher threw a curveball. He told his students about an item he had read in the newspaper that morning concerning a public school in Florida that—in an effort to encourage even greater uniformity in appearance and a concomitant solidarity in school spirit—was requiring all students to adopt similar haircuts: for boys, short "buzz cuts," and for girls, a slightly longer style.

I watched this teacher as he deftly responded to his students' outrage at the proposal by explaining that this was simply an extension of the school uniform principle—encouraging common appearance to improve a sense of solidarity. A bit playfully, he also observed that most teenagers are unnecessarily obsessed with their hair ("Look at me," he said, "mine's almost gone and I still feel fine," and besides—"It'll grow back after graduation.").

Sensing that his point had been made and that students were clearly engaged in the topic, he admitted that such a proposal was in fact not under consideration in Florida. He quickly and emphatically added, however, that some students in France were facing a similar predicament. He explained about the ban on Muslim headscarves in French public schools and suggested to his students that the degree of attachment and identity they feel toward their hair was easily matched by many Muslim females' commitment to wearing the *hijab* in public.

Clearly the Muslim headscarf controversy in France had not been on most students' radars. This ultimately did not prevent them from engaging in thoughtful, reasoned deliberation about the issue and its relevance to broader questions of religious and national allegiance. Efforts toward imaginative engagement will often require more time and exploration than this vignette described, but thoughtful and respectful deliberation would be nearly impossible without them. While some observers might disapprove of the temporary ruse about Florida haircuts, the principle informing this lesson is a powerful one: drawing connections—on both a cognitive and affective level—between perspectives with which students could already relate (extreme school dress codes and intense personal identification with one's hair/style) and unfamiliar ones (intense personal identification with religious garb).

Chapter 3 made a normative claim that respect for others requires mutual understanding, and this assertion forms the basis of my argument for Ethical Dialogue in public schools. But at least some research suggests that an instrumental case can also be made for the value of mutual understanding in the formation of just civic decisions. For example, in her studies of political tolerance among adolescents, Patricia Avery notes that "political experiences appear to expose the individual to a wide range of opinions and attitudes, thereby increasing tolerance for the diversity of beliefs." Here the skeptic will likely question the "thereby"—just because we are exposed to (or even understand) other beliefs doesn't mean we will better tolerate them, does it? But Avery's data provide at least some indication that more understanding is better: tolerant students were far more likely to rely on multiple sources of information in making political judgments. Additional research points to the value of dialogue in which students are encouraged to engage imaginatively with a diversity of ethical perspectives. Students come to recognize and appreciate ethical complexity, and learn to consider information from a variety of sources, avoid overgeneralizations, and resist premature conclusions.[19]

While greater understanding may not always lead to better decisions, it seems doubtful—given the complexity and ambiguity of many ethical issues—that *less* understanding is desirable. Walter Parker offers a vivid illustration here: "To decide solutions to public problems without the advantage of historical and cultural knowledge, and of knowing one another's views, is like trying to rearrange furniture in a dark room."[20] This understanding is multifaceted. It involves knowing one's own position and the reasons for it, as well as which reasons may resonate with someone who disagrees; this in turn involves knowing what objections others might make. This need not reflect an adversarial model in which discussants simply use their understanding of other viewpoints to construct a better argument. It can also involve the joint construction of solutions, which often includes the generation of new ideas through dialogue.

It is vital to understand that grappling with diverse ethical frameworks and their implications for our lives together in society is not the stuff of philosophical esoterica (a point I will continue to argue throughout this book). It may be difficult and controversial, but it is very much a part of our ordinary lives and a frequent (although generally stifled) subtext of classroom discussions. Ethical Dialogue should not be something reserved for "gifted and talented" students any more than civic participation should be restricted to Plato's philosopher kings. Kenneth Strike states the case powerfully:

> We make schools places that deal solely with instrumental goals, but that refuse to deal with matters of central importance to people's lives. We then worry that our children lack commitment to anything of abiding worth. . . . All the while we forget that our society has a rich, sophisticated, and diverse philosophical and religious heritage, one that we seem increasingly unable to transmit to our children. . . . Any education worthy of the name must enable students to deal with questions that are central to human lives in a sophisticated and intelligent way.[21]

There is a rich and growing literature on ways to help students engage with questions of deep meaning. One recent contribution—Katherine Simon's *Moral Questions in the Classroom: How to Get Kids to Think Deeply about Real Life and Their Schoolwork*—offers an inspiring vision of how teachers can foster the type of imaginative engagement I have urged here. We should regularly ask students two basic ethical questions, Simon contends: "What are the implications of what I am learning for my own behavior and beliefs?" and "How does this material help me understand my place in the world?" These are excellent central questions for imaginative engagement, but do not address the tremendously difficult goal of understanding others and learning to deliberate about how to live together in a pluralistic society. Simon acknowledges the importance of learning to "uncover gray area, seek common ground, or build consensus," but this is not the particular focus of her research. Her rich classroom descriptions and suggested pedagogical strategies focus largely on the laudable goals of student self-understanding and expression.[22]

A further step awaits, particularly when considering what needs to be at the heart of civic education. An essential virtue in our pluralistic society is a capacity to reach either consensus or reasonable disagreement, to recognize the reasonableness in positions with which we (even strongly) disagree. As Eamonn Callan contends:

> A schooling system that ignores the deep questions that divide us and stresses instead the increasingly shallow set of substantive values on which almost all of us can currently agree is really contemptuous of who we are because it evades the truth that our identities are deeply implicated in rival answers to ethically divisive questions. A common education for common schools might instead address those questions in a forthright way, while at the same time cultivating a shared reasonableness that would enable us to live together in mutual respect.[23]

This chapter has focused on ways to engage imaginatively with "the deep questions." It is to the cultivation of that shared reasonableness, a process I term *civic deliberation*, that I now turn.

5

Grappling in the Classroom I

Civic Deliberation

The preceding chapter explored the ways in which public school classrooms can help students understand the variety of ethical frameworks in our society through the process of imaginative engagement. While understanding ethical difference is a crucial element in Ethical Dialogue, our role as citizens in a liberal democracy also involves deliberating about those differences as we seek to live together in mutual respect. For example, while my deepened appreciation of your opposing perspective on the death penalty is significant, we may very well still disagree. Recognizing how we disagree isn't enough. The attempt by people to fulfill their differing visions of the good life will frequently result in conflict, and decisions will need to be made about how we will live together.

Obviously, the impact of our life choices on those around us can vary widely. If I feel led to begin each day with a liturgical prayer, or wear a certain head covering, this has minimal impact on others. If my beliefs include the conviction that genetic research is immoral and should be opposed at every turn, however, this obviously involves curtailing the activities of others. Even my commitment to regular prayer might hold implications for those around me, if I request periodic breaks during my workday to pray. It is often more complicated than deciding simply to "live and let live," in spite of this common refrain from students (adolescents in particular, it seems).

If my ethical framework involves the universal prohibition of some aspect of your version of the good life, then mutually respectful deliberation is necessary, and such a skill must be learned. This seems especially true in the consideration of religious truth claims, many of which will be in opposition. Whereas the goal of imaginative engagement is to understand ethical difference, collective deliberation involves navigating the implications of these differences for our lives together. As will become clear, however, this deliberation involves far more than adversarial debate. It seeks to employ the understanding gained via imaginative engagement in a reasoned process supported by mutual goodwill and humility.

The purpose of this chapter is to provide a pedagogic framework for deliberating across ethical differences. At its simplest level, such deliberation rests on two linked assertions:

1. Reasonable people will often disagree about the best way to live.
2. We can recognize that others' views are reasonable (i.e., we can see why they could reasonably think the way they do) and still believe that they are wrong.

The deliberation that emerges from these principles—particularly as it involves religious convictions—relies heavily on crucial distinctions between the realm of our private commitments and our lives together in the civic realm.

THE BIG(GER) TENT OF THE CIVIC SPHERE

To better appreciate the challenge of learning how to deliberate amidst wide ethical diversity, we need to take a brief step back into political theory. As a liberal democratic society, the United States places strong emphasis on both individual rights and collective decision making, and the balance between these two priorities is under constant negotiation. While "liberal" describes our political framework in a general sense, the arguments for weighting individual and communal concerns vary widely within that broad conception.[1]

At this point I need to introduce some key distinctions concerning the idea of the private and civic realms. These terms are used in a variety of ways in everyday language, but for the purposes of my argument, I offer very specific stipulations of their meaning. The private refers to the realm in which our own ethical perspectives, our own ideas about the good life, hold sway and are most often shared by others—the areas of

family, religious groups, communal associations, and so on. The civic is
the setting where our various ethical frameworks interact with those who
do not necessarily share our ethical outlook, where we work out how we
are going to live together in society. Public schools are one of the key elements of this civic realm. Within this civic sphere we must identify an
extremely important *subset*, the political realm. The broader civic realm is
where we seek to express and explore the diversity of viewpoints in our
society—the emphasis here is on understanding and evaluation rather
than on making decisions that invoke the power of the state. This latter
element is the purview of the political realm, which involves the use of
state power in determining how we will live together.[2]

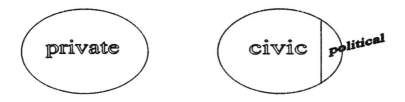

To illustrate these distinctions, consider the common urban issue of
providing transitional housing for prison parolees. In the *private* realm,
a local church or mosque community might discuss their ethical obligation to establish a support center for parolees. The reasons they give for
helping parolees will likely include justifications drawn from their particular religious doctrines and theology. This private conversation will
likely transition into a *civic* discussion with local community leaders,
businesses, and neighborhood associations about the desirability and
details of such a plan. Here, all parties need to make an effort to understand these private rationales of the others and hopefully identify at
least some common ground. Finally, it may involve a more narrowly
political dialogue in which governmental approval (zoning, funding,
etc.) is sought, at which point certain limitations on reason-giving
should be observed, a point I will expand on later in this chapter. Dialogue in each of these three realms has different purposes and requires
different patterns of communication if mutual understanding and
respect are to be achieved.

Why do I emphasize the distinctions between these three realms? It's
important that we recognize that civic speech—how we talk together

about our ethical differences and how to live together respectfully in spite of them—is a far broader realm than simply political. That is, decisions about the use of state power (perhaps to coerce those who disagree) are only a small part of the larger civic dialogue where we share our various ethical perspectives and seek ways to live together in mutual respect. Furthermore, we would do well to recognize that our public schools are a prime setting for this civic dialogue to occur, and for our youth to gain skills in it and commitment to it.

If we accept the basic idea of the civic realm as encompassing our involvement with people whose ethical frameworks differ from ours, then my question here is relatively straightforward: What are the necessary characteristics for virtuous ethical deliberation in public (that is, the civic realm)? This is followed by an equally important question: How can teachers help students develop the skills and attitudes necessary to engage in conversations about how we are to live together?

In light of my more expansive conception of the civic realm as including but not limited to the political, I prefer the term *deliberative reason* to *public reason*, because theorists generally use the latter when considerations of state power are involved. Making decisions about how we live together amidst ethical diversity is not exclusively—or even primarily—a political process, and I think we can benefit from considering the notion of deliberative reason more expansively. The standard liberal view of public reason holds that we need common justification for political power, and this requires that we limit our reasons to those that all reasonable citizens can share. But as chapter 4 argued, this need not—and should not—overshadow the importance of beginning the conversation with efforts toward imaginative engagement.

A commitment to the groundwork of imaginative engagement stands in contrast with the impression given by—if not the actual intent of—many procedural models of deliberative reasoning, in which "gag rules" prohibiting religious arguments are imposed on political discussion.[3] While I will argue that civic virtue involves modulating our political deliberation to some extent, the general lack of consideration of the space between the private and political overlooks the role of imaginative engagement in demonstrating mutual respect and laying the groundwork for just accommodations and compromise.

One prominent advocate of this more restrictive form of liberalism is Stephen Macedo, who seems to consign any efforts toward understanding comprehensive ethics to the private realm. He writes: "The political liberal avoids saying anything about how religion is to be studied: that is left to churches and other private groups. The political liberal can live with the notion that fundamentalism may be the truth in the religious sphere—so long as it does not claim political authority."[4] The separation Macedo prescribes here is too sharp. The civic virtue that Ethical Dialogue seeks to foster cannot remain detached from the study of religion or other important ethical frameworks. As chapter 3 argued, understanding others' ethical frameworks is essential in living together in mutual respect. Furthermore, neither civic nor even the more constrained political deliberation need exclude engagement with such ethical sources; indeed, a fully reasonable analysis requires attention to a wide range of personal beliefs and their implications.

Even when coercive use of state power comes into play on a particular issue, the groundwork for a just decision necessitates abundant civic discussion involving imaginative engagement with reasons we do not all share. Nicholas Wolterstorff offers a compelling rationale for conversation enriched by our varied ethical perspectives.

> Are persons not often worth honoring *in* their religious particularities, in their gender particularities? Does such honoring not require that I invite them to tell me how politics looks from their perspective—and does it not require that I genuinely listen to what they say? We need a politics that not only honors us in our similarity as free and equal, but in our particularities. . . . Cannot the understanding of politics by those of us who do not embrace Judaism be enriched by Judaism's understanding of politics? But how could such enrichment ever take place if, in the public square, we do our best to silence all appeals to our diverse perspectives, regarding the felt need to appeal to them here and there as simply a lamentable deficiency in the scope and power of public reason—a deficiency whose overcoming we hope for?[5]

Wolterstorff's perspective is an appealing one, and it certainly resonates with the chapter 3 argument that respect involves understanding others in their ethical particularities. But before we conclude that political deliberation should be indistinct from broader civic discussion and the imaginative engagement described in chapter 4, the principle of respect for others deserves further consideration. As I will detail in the next section, mutual respect requires that we modulate our deliberative approach in the political realm; in this sense, the political process Wolterstorff criticizes should still be somewhat constrained.

In fact, Wolterstorff himself acknowledges the need for thoughtful and modulated political reason-giving, although his rationale appears to be an instrumental one (i.e., it is necessary for persuasive purposes) rather than based on the assertion that mutual respect requires such accommodation. He observes that if we want to persuade someone who does not accept the reasons we give, we need to find additional reasons. But like many critics of liberal theory, Wolterstorff seeks to remove any a priori filters targeting private ethical frameworks—religious and otherwise—in political deliberation. Underlying this resistance, it would seem, is an optimism about the potential of imaginative engagement to help us reach accord in a way that will allow us to make political decisions largely amenable to discussants. But the hard—and quite obvious—truth of ethical difference is that, at the end of the day, strong disagreement will often remain, and yet some sort of decision (even if it is to preserve the status quo) must be reached. Such a decision may result in the power of the state being used in ways that restrict the liberty of citizens. Unless a deliberative process balances the liberal democratic ideals of majority rule and protection of minority rights, whatever cross-ethical understanding was initially generated will be of little value or relevance to those citizens.

This perhaps unsettling recognition should in no way minimize the value of imaginative engagement, however. The moral authority of difficult political deliberation depends on the inclusiveness of the discourse that precedes it. We do need the opportunity to genuinely communicate and consider our differing ethical perspectives. If we have not cultivated this ground, so to speak, then we have shown inadequate respect to others. In addition, our level of compromise and accommodation may be too shallow to sustain our life together.

What we need is a modulated, deliberative speech that will convey mutual respect in at least two ways: it will recognize and honor the depth of participants' various ethical frameworks while at the same time preserving, as much as possible, the rights of individuals to pursue their own reasonable conceptions of the good. What are the qualities of a deliberative reason that will enable us to demonstrate mutual respect and make decisions about how to live together?

QUALITIES OF DELIBERATIVE REASON

Ethical Dialogue holds that—as a matter of civic virtue[6]—arguments made involving political decisions should adhere to standards of deliberative reason. When considering the qualities of deliberative reason, the notion of what counts as "reasonable" is obviously paramount. As a starting point, I will rely on John Rawls's conception of reasonableness, involving what he terms *reciprocity* and *the burdens of judgment*. The principle of reciprocity requires us to establish and honor fair rules of cooperation. It is a form of mutual goodwill that dissuades us from violating such rules even when it would be to our advantage to do so. Furthermore, my commitment is contingent upon the willingness of others to do the same.[7] For example, if I have exclusive access to information that weakens my argument or strengthens my political opponent's argument, I am obliged to include it in our conversation; my opponent must do likewise. It is worth nothing that reciprocity thus requires the type of mutual understanding described in chapter 3, since we cannot determine whether fair rules have been established if we remain ignorant as to the ethical interests of other participants.

The second element of Rawlsian reasonableness requires acceptance of the burdens of judgment. Accepting the burdens of judgment involves recognizing that reasonable people will disagree about conceptions of the good and the right; it is an inevitable feature of the human condition. Any question involving the use of human reason involves the likelihood that reasonable people will see things differently.[8] This does not mean that all perspectives will be equally valid, but rather that the limits of human reason often prevent a singular answer that is clear to all reasonable parties. In light of this acknowledgment, political-ethical decisions will often require forbearance, compromise, and accommodation involving a range of reasonable frameworks.

This notion of reasonableness—with its basis of mutual respect—is a moral one. This distinguishes it from rationality, the exercise of which can be an entirely self-interested endeavor. While it may at times be rational for me to play fairly as reciprocity requires, my rational motivation is that cooperation will help fulfill my own ends. It may also be rational at times for me to be unreasonable—to reject reciprocity and the burdens of judgment. For instance, it may be entirely rational for me to withhold evidence known only to me that casts doubt on my argument; this violation of reciprocity, however, would be unreasonable. Reasonableness also involves the reciprocal notion that our reasoning is intersubjective—your dignity, your reasons, deserve the same consideration as mine. The value of deliberative reason does not rest on purely procedural grounds, with an assumption that whatever decision is reached will be just. Instead, it requires that decisions—and the preceding dialogue itself—must first abide by these principles of reciprocity and acceptance of the burdens of judgment.[9]

At this point, some readers may question the feasibility of fostering this understanding of reasonableness in precollegiate students. Is this asking students to become philosophers? Stephen Macedo, for instance, argues that concepts such as the "burdens of judgment" are too subtle and complex for all but the most sophisticated high school seniors.[10] But this concern overlooks a crucial distinction: Ethical Dialogue does not require students to understand and accept the philosophical doctrines of reciprocity and the burdens of judgment *as philosophical doctrines*. Rather, students need to recognize the significance of these principles in action and be willing and able to honor them. Ethical Dialogue does not require students to become philosophers, at least in any formal sense of the word. While I find phrases such as "Reasonable Doesn't (necessarily) Mean Right" to be memorable taglines to use with students, the terminology of "reciprocity" and "acceptance of the burdens of judgment" never need be introduced for students to come to appreciate that respectful dialogue involves mutual goodwill, and that reasonable people will disagree about ethical questions.

At the same time, it seems likely that integrating the notion of reasonable disagreement into one's deliberative practice is a developmental achievement. The capacity to recognize the reasonableness of multiple viewpoints first requires the ability to see an issue from multiple perspectives. Research suggests that children in primary grades may have difficulty with the full exercise of reasonable disagreement, although some degree of understanding other perspectives seems possible even for them, as the writings of kindergarten teacher Vivian Paley illustrate (explored later in this chapter).[11] Accordingly, the skills of imaginative engagement should probably be the primary focus of Ethical Dialogue for our youngest students, with the practice of civic deliberation gaining prominence as students develop.

Acknowledging the limits of human reason and accepting the burdens of judgment does not include the idea that all ethical frameworks are equally valid, or even tolerable. As I mentioned previously, some argue that no a priori filters should exist that restrict the kinds of arguments made in political deliberation. We should recognize, however, that such a position is untenable in its extreme formulation. If mutual respect is to serve as the cornerstone of civic virtue, some deliberative standards are unavoidable; in fact, even a political sphere grounded in mere tolerance requires some discrimination regarding which reasons merit full consideration. If our foundation of mutual respect depends in part on avoiding oppression, we must be morally discriminating in the reasons we use for political action. For example, we cannot preserve mutual respect amidst arguments that a particular immigrant group deserves lower entry status simply because of their ethnicity. This does not mean that we always act against those whose views violate the norms of reasonableness—some unreasonable pluralism will be tolerable—but when educating for civic virtue, we need to encourage the practice of reasonableness.

This combination of evaluative humility and robust protection of rights forms the core of deliberative reason necessary for civic virtue. While it may frequently include religiously-informed beliefs about the good life and objective truth, these should be tempered with the acknowledgment that such convictions cannot be fully justified in the political realm. For an argument involving coercion of dissenters to prevail untouched by compromise, it must succeed not only as a compelling argument in and of itself, but it should also establish itself as the only reasonable ethical choice. If we conclude that reasonable disagreement exists about a particular good, then some sort of political compromise should be reached involving these reasonable alternatives.

Here we need to recall a distinction made in the previous chapter, however. The liberal premise of reasonable disagreement and resulting ethical indeterminacy need not mandate a belief in ethical pluralism. As Charles Larmore points out, the ethical pluralist will at least sometimes see such disagreement as evidence of valid but contrasting ethical frameworks, but the monist also has interpretive options. For instance, the monist can argue that only one framework holds the truth, while acknowledging that this truth cannot be politically justified. Alternatively, the monist can coherently maintain that such beliefs are merely different conceptions of what is ultimately a singular source of value.[12] To exemplify this latter stance, consider the principle of mutual respect held by many secular and religious frameworks. A theist might endorse a secular commitment to mutual respect but contend that this justification ultimately rests on humans' status as equal creations of God. This distinction between reasonable disagreement and ethical pluralism is important in emphasizing that the standards of deliberative reason, while demanding, do not exclude ethical monists (many of whom will be religious adherents) from the conversation.

Acknowledging the need for some standards of deliberative reason only gets us so far, however. A common complaint when discussing the requirements of reason is that we have no reliable standards of judgment. Rawls's notions of reciprocity and the burdens of judgment, for example, are criticized for being overly vague. While certainly no guarantee of agreement on the reasonable exists, it would be hard to imagine a just political realm in which the principles of reciprocity and acceptance of the burdens of judgment were rejected by all or even most citizens. To reject these is to reject the very basis of respect for persons, because it denies our basic moral equivalence. Moreover, even if Rawls is wrong to believe that a common reasonableness is enough to generate consensus on a specific conception of justice, such a consensus may not be necessary to a politics of mutual respect; a common reasonableness that serves to constrain the level of moral disagreement over such principles is still a viable and vital element of the civic realm.

In this sense, Ethical Dialogue as an educational philosophy and pedagogical commitment does not stand or fall on a strict Rawlsian exclusion of religious reasons from political decision making. The principles of reciprocity and the acceptance of the burdens of judgment may perhaps be honored through a somewhat looser version of deliberation. The recent work of Jeffrey Stout presents a compelling vision of democracy whose deliberative flexibility is nonetheless rooted in the mutual goodwill and epistemic humility of civic reasonableness.

> Democracy involves substantive normative commitments, but does not presume to settle in advance the ranking of our highest values. Nor does it claim to save humanity from sin and death. It takes for granted that reasonable people will differ in their conceptions of piety, in their grounds for hope, in their ultimate concerns, and in their speculations about salvation. Yet it holds that people who differ on such matters can still exchange reasons with one another intelligibly, cooperate in crafting political arrangements that promote justice and decency in their relations with one another, and do both of these things without compromising their integrity. Cooperating democratic citizens tend also to be individuals who care about matters higher than politics, and expect not to get their way on each issue that comes before the public for deliberation.[13]

While Stout's overall analysis rejects some of the restrictions of political decision making that I support, his depiction of democracy as a profound yet penultimate commitment resonates with the vision of civic virtue embedded in Ethical Dialogue.

Here again it may be useful to emphasize the distinction I have drawn between respect and endorsement. If we think of reasonableness as a sort of civic respect, what we are asking students to do is widen their conception of views that merit this respect. We should make clear to students, however, that this respect need not equate with acceptance or approval. This hearkens back to the importance of imaginative engagement as a precursor to the deliberative process, which seeks to recognize the reasonableness of other views; nevertheless, students are not asked to endorse the ethical frameworks they explore. Will Kymlicka offers a useful summation: "To learn public reasonableness, students must come to know and understand people who are reasonable and decent and humane, but who do not share their religion. Only in this way can students learn how personal faith differs from public reasonableness, and where to draw that line."[14] Public school classrooms are part of the civic realm, as well as vital preparation for it.

ALTERNATIVES TO DELIBERATIVE REASONING

Models of deliberative democracy are not without their critics, of course. Proponents of "communicative democracy," such as Iris Young, argue that the Rawlsian conception of the reasonable is too narrow and creates a process in which participation is surreptitiously limited and formal argumentation unjustifiably privileged. There is much to heed in Young's critique, but I believe the wisest response is to address the potential shortcomings of deliberation rather than discard it as a central feature of Ethical Dialogue.

Just as some observers have criticized modern character education for ignoring many of the underlying social structures and conditions that contribute to injustice (see chapter 2), Young contends that an exclusively deliberative approach often serves to maintain the status quo. Critics of deliberative democracy often point to the apparent assumption of ideal starting conditions for deliberation, marked by equal standing and power of all participants. Obviously, such conditions do not exist. Since participants often occupy different sociocultural positions, the practice of invoking the common good raises questions as to whose good is being championed. But I contend that neither social differentiation nor concern for the common good deserve the blame. Engaging with ethical difference—with the goal of deepening understanding—is the central purpose of imaginative engagement and underscores its essential role in the broader process of Ethical Dialogue. At the same time, a certain commitment to the "common good"—in the form of mutual respect grounded in reciprocity—is absolutely vital if we are to protect the rights of all participants.

What we need, as Natasha Levinson contends, is "a theory of deliberative democracy for unjust conditions. Such a theory would not follow the circular logic in which 'ideal processes of deliberative democracy lead to substantively just outcomes because the deliberation begins from the starting point of justice.'"[15] It certainly makes no sense to encourage Ethical Dialogue as a practical endeavor while assuming an ideal starting point. The groundwork of imaginative engagement I described in chapter 4 seeks to acknowledge and engage with the reality of unjust conditions. Ethical Dialogue must certainly extend beyond procedural deliberation; to the extent that it neglects intensive efforts toward imaginative engagement with difference, it fails to develop the mutual respect necessary to avoid the domination of privilege.

As the preceding section noted, political deliberation is not restricted to a formal, linear process of argumentation. Young's notion of communicative democracy emphasizes this broader conception of dialogue; she argues that we should "conceive the exchange of ideas and processes of communication taking place in a vibrant democracy as far more rowdy, disorderly, and decentered" than deliberative democracy seems to prescribe. She sees the emphasis on critical argumentation as a culturally loaded process, privileging those with access to what Lisa Delpit has called "codes of power." Young specifically suggests three alternative modes of discourse: greeting, rhetoric, and storytelling. All three hold powerful possibilities for expression and all should be welcomed in the deliberative process. At the same time, however, these facets of discourse will be most effectively communicated when linked to a chain of reasoning that would make the most compelling use of these alternative forms of expression.[16]

A wonderful example of the multifaceted nature of Ethical Dialogue is to be found in kindergarten teacher Vivian Paley's *You Can't Say You Can't Play*, in which she describes the ongoing conversation in her classroom about the ethics of inclusion and exclusion as manifested in student play. To encourage student engagement with the issue, Paley weaves a story involving a bird, a princess, and other delightful characters, all of whom wrestle with issues of loneliness and our obligations to others. Elsewhere Paley has observed, "Children, even as young as kindergartners, are devoted to [ethical] inquiry, but to go beyond the fleeting thought, they must meet these important concepts inside a story." To my mind, Paley's classroom models imaginative engagement at its finest, and her narratives serve as a key mode of ethical discourse. But it is worth pointing out that Paley also encourages a more formal analysis of her new dictum "You can't say you can't play." She goes beyond understanding to evaluation and decision making with her students. As she tells one of them, "We're talking about it, getting opinions, thinking about it, wondering how it will work." She regularly probes student reasoning, helps identify conflict and common ground, and helps construct the best cases for and against the proposed rule and whether it can be implemented fairly. Imaginative engagement—through the narrative mode advocated by Young—combines with ethical deliberation here to generate a rich and inspiring lesson for Paley's students.[17]

Paley's masterful teaching also resonates with another prominent version of dialogue, associated with the ethic of care developed by Nel Noddings. This, too, is posited as an alternative to the deliberative process, but—similar to Young's communicative democracy—I believe the philosophy and practice of caring is best conceived as a vital component of broader Ethical Dialogue. Noddings criticizes the tendency for deliberative speech to become adversarial and ultimately counterproductive. She urges an approach to dialogue that emphasizes the importance and value of the participants, an interpersonal reasoning instead of only logical-mathematical. To the extent this approach serves the goal of imaginative engagement, it is a powerful contributor to Ethical Dialogue. The problem, as Eamonn Callan points out, arises when the relationship between participants is valued above the content of the dialogue. Callan elaborates: "I am not more important than the problems of racism, censorship and pornography, sexual responsibility and exploitation, women's reproductive rights and the moral status of the fetus, the requirements of economic justice or any other matter of real moral weight that might arise in thoughtful dialogue between teachers and their students." In Ethical Dialogue, our striving for reasonableness and justified accommodation must remain central. The ethic of care—as it helps nurture both imaginative engagement and respectful deliberation—can play a powerful role in that journey, but we lose something vital if it becomes the goal of the journey itself.[18]

While I believe that the ethics of caring and communicative democracy described here can be accommodated by the broad framework of Ethical Dialogue (particularly as part of imaginative engagement), another prominent alternative to deliberative reasoning takes the form of adversarial, or agonistic, democracy. This general approach actually involves two often linked but importantly distinct ideas: the singular goal of political victory, and confrontational (even belligerent) speech.

The first element of adversarial democracy that sets it apart from deliberation is its disregard for the conditions of reciprocity and acceptance of the burdens of judgment. Whereas deliberation includes dialogue marked by mutual goodwill and acknowledgment that others might reasonably disagree, the fundamental goal of adversarial democracy is political victory through tactical maneuvering. Such an approach has little or no faith in the value of mutual goodwill in reaching just decisions; instead, it assumes that justice is best served by participants doing all they can to promote their own partisan views. But Deborah Tannen cautions against an adversarial framework that "tempts—almost requires us—to oversimplify or even misrepresent others' positions; cite the weakest example to make a generally reasonable work appear less so; and ignore facts that support others' views, citing only evidence that supports our own positions."[19] It is worth noting that these tactics are more or less expected in debate formats, whether taught by the school speech coach or the social studies teacher. In these contexts, listening to one's opponents is only useful in identifying weaknesses and gauging the potential for tactical compromise, not gaining insight into the controversy, recognizing reasonable disagreement, and perhaps moving closer to accommodation or even agreement. While students certainly need practice in framing a convincing argument, developing this skill should not come at the expense of nurturing broader virtues of citizenship and learning from our ethical differences with others.

Nevertheless, there are certainly times when civic virtue must move beyond deliberation to what Young terms democratic activism. She argues that seeking change through political deliberation alone is sometimes insufficient, a charge that history would certainly seem to confirm. Both discussion aimed at persuasion and direct action aimed at protest (and even coercion) are sometimes necessary to achieve justice. The latter may occasionally be necessary when deliberative procedures are designed to protect the status quo.[20] When considering ethical education as a whole, I concur with Young. As I observed in the introduction to this book, Ethical Dialogue is only a part of a broader ethical education, not only in the classroom and broader school context but in the wider community as well. And while actual protest, resistance, and civil disobedience seem less likely in the context of classroom dialogue, their consideration in a historical context constitutes an important example of and lesson in civic virtue. There may well be times in the lives of students and schools—or certainly, as adult members of society—when activism beyond deliberation is called for; an ethical education should help prepare students for that possibility.

One common by-product of an adversarial approach to democracy is a tone of belligerence, a dialogical combativeness entirely dismissive of the type of interpersonal care Noddings advocates. Granted, such a tone sometimes emerges from recognition of an issue's deep moral importance, and for this reason we should not rule out confrontational stances from all Ethical Dialogue. It would be misguided, for example, to expect that critics of child prostitution should soften their indignation and attend more to the relationship with their ideological opponents. But the classroom is a different setting than a political rally, and much is at stake when students are engaged in ethical confrontation. We would do well to remember Robert Nash's repeated admonition when engaging with ethical difference in the classroom: "Proceed with utmost caution at all times." And even regardless of the setting, the limits of our own human reason should give us pause before expressing condemnation of a different ethical perspective. As Cheshire Calhoun observes, "When one is very sure that one has gotten it right, and when avoiding a major wrong is at stake, civility does indeed seem a minor consideration. But to adopt a principle of eschewing civility in favor of one's own best judgment seems a kind of hubris."[21]

While students should be exposed to the possibilities of adversarial democracy, they should also be helped to understand that the absence of a respectfully regulated speech presents significant risks to civility. To many, the notion of civility may seem at best old-fashioned, and at worst slavishness to the status quo. It should be neither, but it does play an important role in Ethical Dialogue. Civility provides structure wherein we can explore disagreement and the discomfort that often accompanies it. The civility we need is active rather than passive, engaging rather than avoiding. Civility does not necessarily require the suppression of passion, but it does involve the recognition that ongoing dialogue is generally best served by avoiding personal attacks, even when individuals can arguably be implicated as part of broader structural injustice in society. It acknowledges the fragility of dialogue involving deep ethical convictions and the vulnerability of its participants, and aims to keep the conversation going even while hard truths are exposed.

Civility should not be merely an artificial etiquette that participants employ within the boundaries of deliberation. Rather, it is nurtured through the groundwork of imaginative engagement and gains value to participants as they seek to understand one another and face the challenges of living together. In my ongoing efforts to foster Ethical Dialogue, I have been struck by how quickly classroom discussion can deteriorate into talk-show-style rhetoric, with participants grabbing the figurative microphone to perform their impassioned and self-righteous soliloquy, with little regard for how their comments might wound those around them. What matters, it seems, is to be heard, to have one's perspectives, feelings, and experiences validated. I recognize the legitimacy of this need, but am convinced that one cannot be heard by a group of people whose only goal is to have *themselves* be heard—no one truly listens, and little regard is paid to the civility necessary to honor the perspectives and feelings of others. I continue to be guided in this respect by the wisdom of Parker Palmer.

> A learning space needs to be hospitable not to make learning painless but to make the painful things possible, things without which no learning can occur—things like exposing ignorance, testing tentative hypotheses, challenging false or partial information, and mutual criticism of thought. Each of these is essential to obedience to truth. But none of them can happen in an atmosphere where people feel threatened and judged.[22]

To make the painful things possible—here lies the connection between growth and safety. A hospitable classroom is not a sufficient end goal, but it is certainly a vital ingredient in helping students grow beyond their necessarily limited experiences. One of the greatest challenges of the teacher's role is to allow room for students' ethical passion while preserving an environment in which students feel safe enough to engage in dialogue, admit ignorance, and learn from one another. The following section suggests some ways in which the grappling of civic deliberation can be encouraged in the classroom.

Deliberative Reasoning in the Classroom

Ethical Dialogue, and even its deliberative component, involves more than debate or even formal argument. It is about reason-giving in its broadest sense, and this sometimes runs counter to the intuitions and practices of teachers, particularly involving the use of students' personal experience in classroom discussion. Veteran teachers know too well the tendency of some students to base all arguments on their (inevitably limited) personal experience, and thus—as researcher Diana Hess has documented in her study of classroom discussion of controversial issues—many teachers do not consider personal experience an acceptable form of deliberative evidence.[23] But just as I have argued that sharing of personal experience should be a welcome facet of imaginative engagement, it also serves an important purpose in the deliberative process by acknowledging that our experiences (particularly to the extent others can identify with them) properly influence how we decide to live together.

Not only is the notion of deliberative reason more expansive than might be assumed, but the process of deliberation includes more than formal argumentation. It can take nonlinear forms, where participants experiment with ideas, repeat and rephrase different perspectives, and pursue apparent tangents as possible new avenues of insight. Ideas evolve and meaning is jointly constructed. From a pedagogical standpoint, it is important to permit and even encourage this somewhat amorphous process. One of my graduate students, a community organizer and social justice advocate who was less familiar with the academic culture of precise argumentation, told me: "Some of us don't have strong analytical skills; Ethical Dialogue needs a language and process that is simple and clear enough to engage and empower people like me." She is absolutely correct, and her assertions are echoed by many critics of deliberative democracy I acknowledged in the previous section. While learning how to develop a carefully constructed argument is an important skill for Ethical Dialogue, it should not come at the expense of spontaneous engagement with the issues and an honest exploration of differing perspectives. As Nel Noddings contends, "Certainly arguments in moral philosophy should interest us. They should help us to detect weaknesses and strengths in our own positions. Also, it seems reasonable to help students learn how to conduct ideal conversation. As we do this, however, we must be careful to guard against sophistry: we do not wish to turn out students who can make the poorer case seem better and the better case seem poorer by their skills in argumentation."[24]

Sometimes this tendency toward sophistry is encouraged by the pedagogical strategies teachers use, such as the common practice of classroom debates. Deborah Tannen points out that teachers often rely on the debate format because it is easy to set up and it seems clear, from the noise and excitement, that learning is taking place. What frequently gets lost, however, is the attitude of reciprocity that reasonableness requires. Genuinely exploring ethical complexities is much harder than simply trying to "win," but ultimately more rewarding. Tannen cites the example of one teacher who has her class compare *three* perspectives, rather than two, to lessen students' tendency to see things in opposition rather than on their own terms.[25]

Another reality of classroom deliberation that the programmed activity of debates sometimes obscures is that facilitating such discussion is frequently more difficult than it appears, requiring detailed and thoughtful preparation on the part of teachers and, ultimately, their students. We should not assume that simply presenting ethical controversies will automatically capture the interest of students; my ongoing efforts in my eleventh-grade English class are testament to this. I won't soon forget the good-natured mocking I received recently when I tried to jumpstart a discussion by stressing how pivotal the debate over Congressional filibustering rules might turn out to be. "Oooh, filibustering, Mr. Kunzman." Eyes rolled, adolescent sarcasm filling the room. "Senate procedural rules—how fascinating!"

Capturing students' attention is only the first step, however, and hardly ensures that a free-flowing, high-quality discussion that deepens students' understanding will emerge. While a deliberative process characterized by informal conversation and gradual iteration is often useful, structured discussion remains an important element of political deliberation. Many experienced teachers will attest to the value of a systematic approach to dialogue, including prior research, full student participation, recapping of main points, and post-discussion evaluation rubrics. Such formal discussion need not be competitive; cooperative elements such as "time-outs" to allow students to help each other can easily be incorporated into the structure. A wide literature exists on the desired qualities of "the deliberative arts" and includes such elements as delineating central value conflicts, identifying common ground, considering relevant alternatives, slowing the rush to judgment, questioning assumptions, drawing analogies, and gaining comfort with uncertainty. Implicit in these qualities, but important to underscore, is the importance of learning to listen well.[26]

One particularly important responsibility of teachers is making sure that students not only have access to the range of reasonable viewpoints on an issue, but striving to ensure that these viewpoints are presented as effectively as possible. The gold standard for this principle, asserts Thomas Kelly, is if the most articulate spokesperson for a particular perspective had been sitting in the back of the classroom, she would have felt her best case was made fairly and accurately.[27] The process of imaginative engagement plays an essential preliminary role here, and (as discussed in chapter 4) many avenues exist to help students appreciate unfamiliar perspectives and their arguments.

Again the skeptic may wonder whether such deliberative discussion is beyond the reach of many students, particularly those who lack advanced verbal and reasoning skills. Will such students be willing and able to step into dialogue and practice the skills of deliberation? Secondary school teachers Alan Singer and Michael Pezone argue they will, citing their own extensive experience in the classroom: "We find that democratic dialogues are much more successful in classrooms with students who are targeted for failure by our society than they are in college-bound classrooms where students compete for grades and the approval of teachers. Generally resistant students readily respond to the opportunity for individual freedom of expression and collective decision making offered by the dialogue process."[28] In my own experience, this is doubly true when the issues being discussed are the deep, vital ones that characterize Ethical Dialogue. The assertion here bears emphasis: students of widely differing levels of academic achievement deserve exposure to and practice with Ethical Dialogue, and while obviously instruction will need to be differentiated, this is no different than most curricula experienced by a heterogeneous school population.

A PORTRAIT OF ETHICAL DIALOGUE

I opened this book by describing a classroom moment early in my career when I sidestepped a discussion of religion, science, and the public square. Here and in the chapter to follow I recount episodes of more successful forays into Ethical Dialogue. My intent in doing so is not to suggest that my pedagogical efforts always generate the engagement and insight of these particular dialogues—as any teacher knows, sometimes discussions fall painfully flat—but to offer a sense of the potential that exists for developing the skills of thoughtful citizenship through ethical exploration.

When my English class discussed *Brave New World*'s image of conveyor belt reproduction and warnings about cloning in the early 1990s, stem cell research was a term unfamiliar to most citizens. Since then, of course, it has become a hotly contested public issue, not only as a policy question itself but as representative of broader tensions involving the purposes and power of genetic engineering. The topic has arisen repeatedly in my classes and serves as a useful illustration of how the notion of "live and let live" is often insufficient. This particular episode I share here also provided me the opportunity to emphasize with students the notion of reasonable disagreement. When stem cell research came up during a sophomore humanities class one semester, I offered a layman's explanation of how advocates see the potential of scientific and medical applications for stem cell research. I then noted that many people, particularly from religious perspectives, are opposed to such experimentation because they see the destruction of the embryo as akin to abortion. Let me take you back to that conversation.

I could tell from her expression that Sharon was getting frustrated with the implications of this resistance. "So what are we supposed to do about this?" she asks. "Should religious people get their way, even if it means delaying cures for diseases?"

"That's a good question," I respond, looking out over the class. "What do you folks think?"

Julia doesn't hesitate. "Hey, if there are more of us religious people than the rest of you, we should get to choose. That's what a democracy is all about."

I often find that one way to examine ethical assertions my students make is to extend them to the level of broader principle. I seize on this opportunity to raise the idea of tyranny of the majority. "Really? So if the majority of voters decided we should kill off the elderly on their eightieth birthdays, would that be the right thing to do?" After a few jokers reply affirmatively for the shock value, everyone in the class admits that this would be immoral and—in the words of one student—"we all have basic rights that no one can take away."

Sarina, who has been quiet thus far, brings us back to our original topic: "But embryos don't have those rights."

"Why not?"

"They're not people. They can't think, they can't survive on their own. Just because you want to save some microscopic little embryo, you're going to tell all these sick people, "Too bad, you'll just have to die"? I'm not going to listen to some religious nut who values a fetus over a living person!"

I make a mental note to address Sarina's disparaging language later, but don't want to lose the chance here to push the implications of her assertion. "Remember, though, we've all got to play by the same rules of discussion, and we've talked before about trying to understand opposing arguments if we want to get anywhere productive. I understand why you see a big difference between a sick adult and an embryo, but think about many of the Alzheimer's patients who we're trying to save through genetic research—they can't survive on their own, right? And at advanced stages of the disease, we can't recognize any sign of thinking in these patients. Does that mean they no longer have rights?"

Richard jumps in. "No, we can't say that. But then how do we figure out who or what deserves protection?"

From their wandering looks, I sense I'm starting to lose a few as the discussion turns more theoretical. I try to push them further along this line of questioning, but to no avail. Fortunately, Jay brings them back with a personal example and concrete question. "My grandfather died two years ago from Alzheimer's," he says, "but I know he was against abortion because he thought fetuses deserved the same protection as the rest of us. Aren't there other ways of doing this research that don't use embryos?"

Now we're approaching the limits of my offhand scientific knowledge. "Well, it's not entirely clear, but many researchers suspect that embryonic stem cells have more potential for disease research than other kinds of stem cells."

Sarina jumps back in. "But that's the problem, right? We won't know if that's true if embryonic research is limited."

"Good point." I try to help them take stock of the discussion thus far. "OK, so it seems that the heart of the issue is whether embryos have the same rights as people. If you think they do, then the government should strictly limit or prohibit embryonic stem cell research. If you think they don't, then the government should mostly stay out of the way." I pause and scan for looks of comprehension, then introduce a bit more complexity to the question. "So is the controversy just about these two completely opposed viewpoints?" I don't get much in the way of a response here, so I try to direct their thinking a bit more. "Anybody read *Brave New World* yet?" I see a few nods. "Remember how human reproduction worked in that society?"

Grace makes the connection for me and throws in a pop culture reference that flicks a switch for her classmates. "The conveyor belt! Way too spooky—it's like those pre-cogs in Minority Report—genetic mutants who get abused by the government."

Carl laughs in disbelief. "Some science fiction freaks you out and now you want to prevent scientists from finding cures for disease?"

Brian feeds off Carl's indignation. "Yeah, it'd be crazy to hold back scientific research! Even if you could do it, it wouldn't be fair to all the people who have Parkinson's or Alzheimer's and need help."

"But doesn't our society hold back scientific research now?" I ask.

"What do you mean?"

"Well, we have all sorts of standards for how research is conducted that end up slowing down the process. For instance, it takes a long time before drugs can be tested on human subjects." I want them to start to recognize that any functioning society has to put limits on people, has to set boundaries on issues that affect fellow citizens. We've covered a lot of ground quickly here and I decide it's a good time to look back over the terrain. In these situations, I often find it useful to stop and identify any common ground, both to summarize and help us decide where to move on from there. "So up to this point, what do we seem to be agreeing about?"

It takes a few false starts, but eventually we compose a short list on the board: (1) We all want to find cures for diseases; (2) Using adult stem cells is acceptable; (3) Scientific research should have some rules. As I finish writing down this third one, it becomes clear from murmurs of dissent that some people aren't convinced. Sharon draws us back to something similar to her original question: "But who gets to decide what the rules for research should be?"

Emma, who had suggested this final point of common ground, responds. "Well, the government's got to come up with some rules, right? If they don't, it'll be totally unregulated and then there'll probably be some psychos who totally abuse the process. That's what happened with those horrible medical experiments the Nazis did."

I decide we need to think about this idea some more. "One thing I think might be helpful is for us to get a better sense of what could go wrong—and what already has gone wrong—when science and medicine are unregulated. And don't think this just happens in places like Nazi Germany. Did you know your very own state was the first one to force people to get sterilized if the government thought they weren't fit to have children? Tomorrow I'll bring in some information about that, and about a medical study called the Tuskegee Experiment. I'll also see if I can dig up some statements by experts on different sides of the stem cell issue. Tonight I want you to make a list of all the questions you would need answered before you could make a confident decision about the best policy for embryonic stem cell research. Hopefully we can fill in some of the gaps tomorrow."

Clearly, these were just the beginning stages of an Ethical Dialogue.²⁹ The class period ended with a recognition that we needed more information in order to better appreciate the different arguments. While we could certainly gain a better understanding of the issue with a little more research, I also wanted students to come up with these lists so they would begin to realize that many of their pivotal questions (e.g., at what point in the developmental process do we start to deserve full protection as human beings?) don't have clear answers. Instead, there might be multiple *reasonable* ways of formulating a position, and thus the possibility of reasonable disagreement.

Not surprisingly, several more days of exploration and discussion interspersed between other activities resulted in my students still holding a range of opinions about the issue. Ethical Dialogue need not—and usually will not—result in an obvious singular agreement. The diversity of reasonable ethical frameworks renders that outcome unlikely. But this inconclusiveness should not provoke discouragement or lead us to conclude that Ethical Dialogue serves little practical purpose. The process of recognizing the reasonableness of other positions—even while still disagreeing with them—and identifying common ground provides useful starting points for generating compromise and respectful accommodation.

There will, of course, be some highly contentious issues wherein little common ground seems to exist. Skeptics of Ethical Dialogue will contend that many controversies are "too hot to handle" and are more likely to generate counterproductive, emotional divisiveness than compromise and accommodation. I would certainly concede this possibility regarding certain issues in particular contexts (discussing Mideast turmoil with a classroom of Jewish and Arab-American students, for instance). But this critique also serves to point out that Ethical Dialogue is best conceived as an incremental process, where the skills and dispositions involved are cultivated through discussion of less volatile issues, and a degree of mutual trust is developed over time. This latter notion of "civic friendship" can also be nurtured through activities other than Ethical Dialogue, such as groupwork inside the classroom and extracurricular opportunities outside it. Such friendship, however, is not a fully sufficient element of respect amidst deep ethical conflict, as it does not require understanding of others' ethical frameworks as I have described it in the preceding chapters. Nevertheless, civic friendship combined with ongoing exposure to Ethical Dialogue seems an oftentimes valuable precursor to grappling with severe ethical controversy.

Walter Parker describes how the ancient Greeks used the term "idiots" to signify those whose commitment to their own private interests overwhelmed and undermined their commitment to the common good. He points out that this need not be an entirely individualistic stance—families, such as the Mafia, can be idiotic in this sense, enjoying a strong moral code privately but seeing outsiders as beyond any sort of obligation.[30] We might also see how religious affiliation might fall prey to this all-encompassing concern for private commitments and priorities. While the stem cell research vignette I shared earlier did to some extent draw on religiously-informed ethical perspectives, it had the potential to become even more complicated had we pursued more closely a related question such as "Is it fair to let religious convictions shape our lives together in society?" This chapter, while laying out some basic principles of "grappling with the good," did not explore the role and influence of religion specifically on the deliberative process. These are the challenges I will now take up in chapter 6.

6

Grappling in the Classroom II

The Role of Religion

While acknowledging reasonable disagreement is a central virtue of democratic citizenship, Ethical Dialogue also seeks to help participants identify common ground and potential for compromise. Americans appear increasingly unwilling to seek common ground, however, especially with issues informed by religious perspectives. When asked in 2004 whether deeply religious elected officials should vote based on their religious views or be willing to compromise, a majority of Americans who attend religious services at least once a week chose the former. According to the same survey, nonreligious Americans were also increasingly unwilling to compromise on such issues. These findings represented dramatic increases from just four years prior.[1]

An entire book could be written speculating on the root causes of this unwillingness to compromise; not surprisingly, people blame their ideological opponents for the initial intransigence, to which they are simply responding in kind. What *does* seem clear, however, is that as a society, we are not very good at talking across disagreements informed by religion. Consider these survey results in light of a 2004 decision by administrators at Fort Mill High School in South Carolina to remove same-sex marriage and stem cell research from the scheduled topics of a student-run debate. They feared that state laws prohibiting health class discussion of abortion and homosexual sex would carry over to similar topics and other discussion formats.[2] While Americans recognize religion as influential in many people's political views, this very factor of religion—and our disagreement or uncertainty about the role it should play in the public square—makes us shy away from the discussion altogether, especially in public schools.

The preceding chapter explored the idea of civic deliberation—how we talk and make decisions about our lives together—in Ethical Dialogue. But as chapter 3 emphasized, we cannot adequately explore ethical issues without considering how they are informed by various religious perspectives. This chapter addresses the challenges embedded in bringing religion into Ethical Dialogue and the part it should play in civic deliberation.

RELIGION IN THE CIVIC REALM

When discussing and making decisions about how people will live together amidst inevitable disagreement about "the good life," what role should religion play? In his recent book *Religion and the Obligations of Citizenship*, Paul Weithman makes a compelling case that churches and other religious organizations play a vital and under-recognized role in the civic sphere. He introduces the concept of "realized citizenship," arguing that individuals must both *identify* with their citizenship (thinking of themselves as having the rights, interests, duties, and powers of citizens) and have the resources of skills, information, and influence to *exercise* this citizenship. Weithman claims that religious involvement helps many Americans "realize" their citizenship. He provides empirical data showing that churches and other religious institutions foster voter participation more effectively than any other American institution. Beyond voting, Weithman cites research that suggests that this involvement encourages participation in local politics and provides egalitarian opportunities to acquire and practice civic skills (far more than labor unions, interestingly). Weithman places particular emphasis on the role of religious organizations in providing *equality* of opportunity; the contribution of African American churches is especially prominent in this regard.[3]

Beyond the significance of increasing political enfranchisement itself, the implications here for the texture of this citizenship are worth considering. As Weithman acknowledges, religious institutions will naturally provide participants with *religious* reasons for action and foster a conception of citizenship that resonates with *religious* ideals and duties. He does not see this as problematic, since he views religious justifications as fully sufficient for political deliberation.[4]

As I will explain more fully later in the chapter, however, this picture of citizenship as directed almost entirely by religious convictions does conflict with the vision of civic virtue embodied in Ethical Dialogue. But despite my disagreement with Weithman's broader vision of democratic citizenship, the connection he draws between religious commitment and civic participation should not be overlooked. To the extent that Weithman is correct in asserting that religious affiliation and involvement create the sole route by which some participants realize their citizenship, then Ethical Dialogue can play a valuable role in *enlarging* their conception of democratic citizenship. Here we return to the vital distinctions between private, civic, and political; while a student's private (religious) commitments may be pivotal in the "realization" of her citizenship, we should then help her recognize that this citizenship operates in a broader civic realm where mutual respect requires us to engage thoughtfully with ethical difference as we live our lives together. Weithman's argument also reminds us that our Ethical Dialogue should be welcoming of those religiously-informed perspectives, so the connection can be made between the source of their citizenship and the broader civic virtue our democracy requires.[5]

Teachers who encourage Ethical Dialogue in their classrooms will sooner or later face the prospect of navigating religiously-informed ethical positions, ones either raised by students or naturally embedded in the discussion topic. I have found that this challenge arises sometimes even when my intended focus is quite different. For example, in a tenth-grade English course I used to teach, it emerged during a discussion of *Oedipus Rex*. One of the themes I always like to explore in this ancient drama is fate or destiny, not only because it was a central concern of the Greeks, but because my students generally find it an interesting brain stretcher themselves. It pushes them to think about big ideas and questions without clear answers. The drama by Sophocles revolves around a prophecy that Oedipus would kill his father and marry his mother. To foil the prediction, his royal parents abandon him as an infant in the mountains, but he is rescued by foreigners and unwittingly returns to his homeland as an adult, where he, ignorant of the prophecy, fulfills it to every dreadful detail. Let me now step back into that tenth-grade classroom discussion that this ancient drama inspired.

After we finish the story's final page, I drop a question on my students that I hope pushes them to consider the broader question of human responsibility: "So if Oedipus's story was fated to happen from birth, can we really blame him for his actions?"

Albert, a confident student who frequently gets discussions rolling, is the first to respond: "No, he couldn't help it. It's not like he knew that it was his father he attacked, or that his mother was the queen. The only reason he got himself in that mess was because he was running away to avoid the prophecy."

Vivian is willing to challenge this line of thinking. "Yeah, but if Oedipus didn't have such a bad attitude, he wouldn't have attacked his father in the first place."

I want to clarify the contrast in their thinking here, so I follow up: "So Vivian, you think that it was at least partly due to Oedipus's character flaws that this tragedy occurred? He was really to blame?"

Before Vivian can respond, Albert jumps back in. "But it would have happened some other way then. You can't escape your destiny."

I'm about to point out that Vivian didn't have a chance to answer, but Claudio blurts out an idea that I can't leave hanging. "That's true," he says, "Sometimes it's just God's will and there's nothing you can do about it. That's what my mother said when her cousin died of a heart attack when he was only fifty."

"You know, that outlook on fate is pretty similar to many of the Greeks," I point out, "but it's not just some religions that look at life that way. Just a few years back, some scientists argued that we were entirely products of our genetic makeup. Whatever genes we had absolutely determined our behavior."

Unless everyone is sleeping with their eyes open, I'm pretty sure someone will contest this, and Deanna comes through for me. "That's ridiculous. I'm in charge of my life and I make decisions about the kind of person I want to be." Then she adds for good measure, "People who argue 'God made me do it' or 'the devil made me do it' or plead temporary insanity are copping out!"

I realize I can transition us right there into a discussion of how religion influences our world together, but the idea of framing our discussion of religion in terms of Jim Jones or Charles Manson is more than I want to attempt in the final minutes of class. But one of the concepts I *do* want to introduce in this unit is existentialism, and Deanna's assertion is a close enough parallel to draw the connection. (A few years prior, introducing a philosophical idea such as existentialism seemed to me too great a stretch for high school sophomores, until a colleague convinced me that it was a perfect developmental fit for the kinds of questions adolescents were mulling over anyway.) I give them a basic summary of the concept and then decide to invite further connections with their lives and the ethical frameworks that surround them. I tell them that for homework, they need to write an initial position paragraph on existentialism—do you agree with it? why or why not?—and ask their parents what they think about it as well. I'm guessing that at least some students will show up in class next time with religiously-informed views on fate or destiny, so I do a quick reference check that night. I find that many religions, including Christianity, Islam, and Judaism, generally navigate a theology somewhere between free will and fate (predestination).

The next day I decide to pick up again with Deanna's confident assertion about her control over her life. "We spent the last part of class yesterday talking about whether fate or destiny plays a role in our modern lives like it did in the world of Sophocles. Deanna, you argued that appealing to or relying on some sort of divine fate is a cop-out. I'm wondering, a cop-out from what?"

"It's like we talked about in Ms. Taylor's class about the reasons people gave for colonialism. Great Britain and other empires claimed they were bringing the great Christian civilization to the savages. It's pretty easy to do whatever the heck you want when you can say that God is on your side and making it happen."

Eliza jumps in. "That's true. Look at people like David Koresh and Jim Jones. They ruined a lot of lives with that line."

So much for my plans to stay away from religious extremism. It occurs to me that this would be a good time to emphasize the importance of charitable interpretation, of attributing the best possible motives and arguments to a particular perspective, so as to meet it on its most compelling terms. "OK, it would be hard to argue that some notions of divine destiny don't contribute to destructive ends, but before you reject the entire outlook as unreasonable, try looking at it like this. If you believe in a god who has the power to affect events in the world, and is infinitely powerful, is it so out of the question to think that such a god might influence events in a way that are out of our control or understanding?"

This strikes a chord with one student, at least. "That's right—when I asked my father last night, he said that God works in the world all the time, but usually we are too proud to see it," says Julia. "He said he believes that God is going to work His will in the Supreme Court nomination so that righteousness will be brought back to America."

Now we're in the thick of it. I decide to plunge ahead to see if we can grapple with these central dilemmas about our lives together. "This raises a larger question I think it's important for us to think about. Is it a good idea to let religious beliefs shape the way our society looks?" I pause for a moment before rephrasing. "What I mean is, should people let their religious views shape how we all live together and the laws we make?"

On the one hand, this is a complex question. On the other hand, I find that students almost always have opinions about it. Eliza shares first: "Part of me wishes we could just rule all that religious stuff out, but I don't see how it's possible, Mr. Kunzman. How are you going to tell Julia's dad that he can't vote the way his religion tells him to?"

"No way that's going to happen," says Julia, shaking her head.

"OK, good point," I concede. "But it's one thing to let religious beliefs tell you how *you* should vote or push for policies, and another thing to expect nonbelievers to see your religious beliefs as valid reasons to go along with what you want, right?"

I'm not sure if they're tracking at this point, and thankfully Albert is willing to admit it. "I don't get it," he says. "What's the problem? Everyone has their reasons."

I pull an example from the headlines, one most of them have seen, even if they don't know the details. "Imagine you're an atheist, and you support the legislation that's currently in our state assembly to grant legal marriage rights to same-sex couples. Let's assume for a minute that the representative who's leading opposition to the bill bases his argument on his interpretation of the Protestant Bible, and claims that homosexual practice is against God's law and therefore it should be against our laws, too. Now remember, you're the atheist—what are you going to say to that?"

Albert plays along. "I'm going to say that his reasons are lame. Why should I believe his interpretation of the Bible, or believe the Bible at all? He's got no proof."

"Right, and he's going to say that you don't need proof to believe the Bible, you need faith. He's got faith, and if you had faith, you'd see the truth of what he's saying."

I hear a few yelps of frustration at this point. If nothing else, they are seeing how difficult this can be. Gwen speaks slowly, formulating her question as she goes. "But if you can't provide any real evidence . . . how are you going to convince anyone of your beliefs?"

I want to acknowledge their frustration here but also raise the question of what we mean by evidence, what we mean when we say that someone is making a good argument. "I guess part of it depends on what counts as 'real evidence.' So this kind of returns us to my question, because if we disagree on what counts as evidence, as good reasoning, because of our differing religious beliefs, it's going to be tough to find common ground."

Our discussion did not end here, but before I relate the second half of the vignette, this question of whether religion can be reasonable, and what civic virtue requires of religious adherents who bring their convictions into civic deliberations, needs further analysis.

CAN RELIGION BE REASONABLE?

The preceding chapter, in describing the qualities of deliberative reason, suggested that virtuous political deliberation needs to be regulated. Here the nature of this regulation receives closer scrutiny: to what extent does this place limits on the justifications offered by many religious-ethical frameworks?

The deliberative reasoning I advocate as part of Ethical Dialogue is not an ethically neutral language, despite claims to the contrary by some theorists. Attempts to construct a "thin" political liberalism inevitably require a more comprehensive bulwark of beliefs about the good, and this implies conflict with at least some conceptions of the good life. Veit Bader puts it bluntly: there is a "price to be paid for living in modern societies and under liberal-democratic constitutions." The price, as it manifests in Ethical Dialogue, is a limit on the arguments we should make when the coercion of others is at stake. Since some ethical frameworks fit more easily within the boundaries of reciprocity and burdens of judgment, these limits will unavoidably impinge on some frameworks more than others. These restrictions do not constitute disrespect for others, however. Rather, they help safeguard a social environment in which respect can flourish. The notion of a fully neutral political realm in which everyone is fully respected and yet all ethical frameworks are entirely acceptable is incoherent.[6]

The relationship between liberalism's discriminating deliberative language and religious languages, however, seems widely misunderstood. Some theorists appear to equate *reasonable* with *secular*, and thus *religious* with *unreasonable*. From an epistemological standpoint, this is simply mistaken. Plenty of secular reasons are unreasonable, and many religious reasons are reasonable. As Richard Baer observes, "There are no reasonable epistemological standards that allow us to judge theological thinking as inherently inferior or less reliable than secular or non-theistic thinking."[7]

One could grant this epistemological point, however, and still argue that much religious-ethical reasoning is destined to violate the boundaries of reasonableness. For instance, Eamonn Callan argues that even "sophisticated" religious believers intent on civic virtue will have great difficulty squaring the ethics of a determined faith with the civic virtue of restraint in political deliberation:

> Sophisticated believers think that certain things are true with an assurance that self-consciously goes beyond the limits of the reasonable. But they also think it would be wrong to draw on these convictions in political argument, at least about constitutional essentials and basic justice, because doing so would transgress the same limits. That is a high-wire act.

Believers try to balance between keeping religious convictions separate from political judgments and still maintaining those firm convictions for nonpolitical purposes. Callan claims such balance is too difficult to maintain, but I contend that his interpretation is excessively pessimistic. Why must a religious adherent's recognition that others will reasonably disagree with her (acceptance of the burdens of judgment) eat away at her religious creed? Callan asserts that "to retain a lively understanding of the burdens of judgment in political contexts while suppressing it everywhere else would require a feat of gross self-deception that cannot be squared with personal integrity."[8] He seems to question the coherence of the self that says, "I believe *x* to be true because God/Scripture says so, but I recognize that others might reasonably think otherwise, and it would be disrespectful to force them to live in accordance with my belief system."

Callan's model of human psychology strikes me as empirically dubious. It is quite feasible, for example, for a religious adherent to base her opposition to euthanasia on religious grounds and to express these beliefs in the public square as part of ongoing dialogue. Still, she realizes it would violate the principle of respect for others to politically coerce them on that basis. It would not evince a lack of civic virtue, however, to explore other rationales acceptable to her ethical framework and voice these as grounds for political action (even while she maintains a rationale and motivation that are primarily religious). For instance, she might contend that euthanasia would erode society's already deplorable devaluing of people with severe mental or physical disabilities.

Callan's picture of religious commitment itself relies too heavily on a dualism between faith and doubt. He contends that in order to avoid succumbing to doubt, religious believers must rely on "a tenacious assent to dogma which is resistant to the persuasive force of counter-evidence and argument." The validity of Callan's claim rests largely in the meaning of "tenacious." If it involves a continual stonewalling against a rational-critical analysis of religious belief, then Callan's argument for the gulf between religious adherence and civic virtue is compelling. But I think this underestimates the complexity of much religious faith, and not simply that of liberal Protestants. Trevor Cooling points out that basing ethical stances on religious belief can be quite rational—even when we recognize that such belief doesn't provide a fully adequate explanation—if no better explanations are available to us. What is irrational, Cooling claims, would be refusing to see the lack of perfect clarity as significant. Trust, faith, and belief need not equate with a certainty that preempts critical analysis and the "very powerful residual doubts" which Callan rightly suggests such analysis may provoke.[9]

I want to emphasize that my goal in this book is not to argue a normative view of religion, to show how we could make a certain adaptation of religion "fit" within the political bounds of liberal democracy. While at times I offer observations concerning how some major religions can accommodate the principles of Ethical Dialogue within their ethical structures, the primary thrust of my argument addresses what *civic virtue* requires in an ethically diverse, liberal-democratic society. How can and should we learn to talk and live together in light of our ethical differences? The price to be paid for living in a liberal democracy is not to relinquish religious ethics in favor of secular ones. Rather, the price that civic virtue demands is to abide by the limits of our common deliberative reason in our lives together, which in turn will help preserve space in the private *and* civic realms for religious-ethical perspectives to be heard and considered. But as I have shown, these limits do not coincide with the distinction between religious and secular ethics.

Not only should we avoid dismissing religiously-informed arguments as inherently unreasonable, we might also recognize that religious adherents can serve as important models of civic virtue. Religious adherents in liberal democracies are asked to live in multiple worlds of meaning, holding a kind of dual citizenship; in this regard, they can lend insight into the challenge of negotiating the movement between private and political that all of us, in a deeply pluralistic society, must face to some extent.[10] For example, a religious student can demonstrate a valuable lesson to her classmates as she thoughtfully engages with ethical difference—even acknowledging the reasonableness of some positions in conflict with her own deeply held religious-ethical framework. Such a model can demonstrate the vital distinction between the civic realm (where she gives full expression to her private ethical framework) and its political subrealm (where she demonstrates willingness to compromise as reciprocity and the burdens of judgment require).

While a dual commitment to religion and civic virtue can provide an inspiring example to others, we should not underestimate what public life in an ethically diverse society requires of us. Some religious creeds *will* violate the norm of reasonableness required for political coercion, and any argument that seeks to involve religious perspectives more fully in political deliberation must contend with that inevitability. Certainly there will be citizens who refuse to honor reciprocity and accept the burdens of judgment, relying solely on tactical politics. As I acknowledged at the outset of this section, the language of reasonable political deliberation is not neutral. Students—religious and otherwise—need to learn to recognize the limits that reasonableness places on their deliberation, but do so in the context of genuine respect and understanding of religious and other ethical frameworks. This entails students learning not only about standards of reasonableness, but developing a civic commitment to abiding by them in political decisions even when they diverge from their own visions of the good life.

FALLIBILISM AND ETHICAL ADHERENCE

Acceptance of the burdens of judgment—as a necessary component of political deliberation—involves the acknowledgment that one's ethical framework is one of multiple reasonable possibilities. Here, religious believers who hold a strongly exclusivist, fundamentalist perspective toward matters of belief and interpretation will likely object. Asking students to concede this, they would claim, encourages a fallibilism about their beliefs that is unacceptable: it threatens the stability of their faith and questions the very authority of their god.

It is vital here to understand the nature and degree of fallibilism required for acceptance of the burdens of judgment. If by fallibilism we

mean an approach that continually calls into question one's most fundamental, metaphysical beliefs, then such a "strong" fallibilism is not necessary for civic virtue. Rather, students should be willing—in light of reasonable disagreement—to revisit their *application* of core ethical beliefs to
civic matters. This willingness does not preclude acting upon one's convictions for fear that one's civic judgments might possibly change, nor
does it mean insisting that all such perspectives are held only provision-
ally. Such a "weak" fallibilism will not satisfy all religious adherents, of
course, but it does provide more room for religious-ethical frameworks
than some might fear.

To begin with, a student who recognizes the reasonableness of ethical perspectives different from her own is not thereby compelled to with-
draw (or even soften) her assertions and convictions about the truth of
her own framework. In accepting the burdens of judgment, Charles Larmore contends,

> We need not suspend judgment about the correctness of our own views.
> We may still rightfully believe that, despite being controversial, they are
> better supported by experience and reflection than those of our oppo-
> nents. This is because we can recognize that a view is reasonable, yet
> false: it may have been arrived at sincerely and in accord with generally
> accepted forms of reasoning, yet against the background of existing
> beliefs that our own viewpoints judge as false.[11]

Here we return to the student-friendly phrase, "Reasonable doesn't mean
right." If we neglect to make this distinction between reasonableness and
truth, we are faced with a version of fallibilism that requires us to view
even our deepest convictions as tentative. This is asking too much, and
not only of fundamentalist religious adherents; it seems more than a little
deceptive (perhaps toward oneself, but certainly toward others) to claim
that I am willing to call into question even my deepest ethical convictions
whenever I am presented with differing perspectives. In this sense, I
depart significantly from some advocates of interreligious dialogue who
contend that genuine dialogue requires us to hold our entire ethical
framework open to revision. Teachers need not—and should not—
endorse such a vision of risk-all dialogue, or cultivate the impression in
their students that all their beliefs should be continually "up for grabs."[12]

At the same time, we should not conclude that fallibilism has no relevance to recognizing reasonable disagreement. Acceptance of the burdens of judgment involves not only a recognition of the *limits* of human

reason but also its *value*. The need for fallibilism and the concurrent value of human reason in Ethical Dialogue emerges from a very basic notion that, as finite human beings, our grasp of knowledge is necessarily limited. Even religious believers who claim access to the infinite through divine guidance will generally acknowledge that the space between this divine source and themselves is significant. While acknowledging that we will never completely agree on ethical truth—much less that our human reason will achieve it in any objective sense—we must have confidence in our ability to reason together *toward* the truth. To reject this capacity is to despair of the possibility of even distinguishing the reasonable from the unreasonable; without this, our foundational commitment to respect others becomes impossible, since we have no reliable measure of what constitutes disrespect.

To the extent that we recognize the value and importance of human reason, we cannot be content with an attitude that says, "I know I have the truth and—in spite of your admittedly reasonable arguments to the contrary—I know my application of it to how we live together is without error." Acceptance of the burdens of judgment requires us to pay greater heed to reasonable disagreement than that. We need not view human reason as fully sufficient, but we do need to see it as a vital aid in our lives together. To the extent that citizens view human reason as a fruitless search for answers in contrast to their own divinely-informed certainty, they have rejected the civic virtue necessary for Ethical Dialogue.

So while the fallibilism necessary for reasonable disagreement may not prove amenable to certain extreme versions of fundamentalism, it is also important to understand that it need not threaten students' core metaphysical beliefs. Acceptance of the burdens of judgment, we should keep in mind, is a *civic* virtue. This realm is not directly concerned with private metaphysical or creedal beliefs in and of themselves (e.g., the existence of God) but rather the *implications* of those beliefs for public policy. In this regard, students need to have a sense of fallibilism to the extent of recognizing the interpretive distance between their source(s) of truth and their application to how we live together in society. There is no inherent contradiction between adherence to a particular ethical framework and open dialogue about the implications of that framework for the political realm. A significant difference exists between requiring a fallibilism about John's core metaphysical beliefs and encouraging John to recognize that others reasonably believe otherwise and thus will critique his perspective. It should not be the role of the public schools to encourage students to question their most basic metaphysical beliefs, but at the same time students need to learn how to analyze the *implications* of their beliefs and how they appear to and affect other members of the polity.

Acceptance of the burdens of judgment requires us to acknowledge the reasonableness of other ethical stances and modulate our political arguments and decisions accordingly, but this requirement of proportionality does not extend to our ethical frameworks themselves. By this I mean that Maria's acknowledgment of the political reasonableness of Jason's "pro-choice" position on abortion in no way requires her to lessen her conviction that God exists and knits us together in the womb. It is still entirely rational—and civically virtuous—for Maria to maintain a completely committed faith in God.[13]

It is also important for teachers—and, by extension, their students—to recognize that fallibilism does not require a constant revising of one's ethical framework. In fact, it does not necessarily require revision at all; deliberation can also quite reasonably result in ethical *adherence*. "Autonomous revision and adherence are twin facets of the one virtue," Eamonn Callan contends, "and neither is inherently more laudable than the other." The value of holding fast to one's ethical commitments amidst doubt and tribulation, while certainly not absolute, should not be discounted. While Ethical Dialogue prizes an ongoing commitment to learning how to live together, it should refrain from the message that ethical conviction is like an outer garment to be changed with every shift in the social weather. As William Galston cautions, "The greatest threat to children in modern liberal societies is not that they will believe in something too deeply, but that they will believe in nothing very deeply at all."[14]

Perhaps the most prominent philosophical voice to encourage deeper curricular engagement with religion has been Nel Noddings, particularly in her book *Educating for Intelligent Belief or Unbelief.* While I appreciate her advocacy of robust exploration of religion in the classroom, I believe that the orientation she describes is ultimately detrimental to the hope of Ethical Dialogue in public schools. The curricular approach Noddings develops most fully in her book involves a process of examining the "strong points" and "weak points" of an assortment of religions and other ethical frameworks, and then choosing the best fit for oneself. In so doing, Noddings characterizes religious commitment as something readily—and unproblematically—subject to customization and revision (a narrow conception of religion I criticized in chapter 3).[15]

To return to the distinctions I drew at the beginning of chapter 5, Noddings advocates an education that encourages students to judge the value of religions as they manifest in the *private* sphere. In contrast, I believe that public schools should focus on helping students consider the role of religion in the *civic* sphere, where we live our lives together. Part of this education should include an appreciation for the difference between making private choices about our religious commitments and seeking to extend those convictions to our broader society. As I have emphasized already, this is not to argue that there is no place for the expression and advocacy of religious beliefs in the public square; on the contrary, the centrality of such convictions in many citizens' lives means that they will undoubtedly surface in civic deliberation. Ethical Dialogue focuses on the ways in which those commitments must be communicated, negotiated, and respected in the public square. With the focus shifted to the implications for our lives together—rather than on the question of religious truth itself—the vital role of critical thinking and the need for fallibilism may be less problematic for many religious adherents.

As I have suggested, the doctrine of reasonable disagreement—and Ethical Dialogue more generally—will likely hold little value for believers who insist that they have direct, unmediated access to divine truth, who are unwaveringly convinced that they share, in essence, the Mind of God. But between a rootless ethical wandering and the certitude of Mind of God Believers lies a vast territory, one that is inhabited by most religious adherents in the United States. Toward the liberal side are those believers who readily adjust their doctrines in response to shifting social conditions and broader ethical sentiment. Obviously, this responsiveness meshes well with the degree of fallibilism necessary for genuine Ethical Dialogue. But even toward the conservative end of the spectrum, room exists for Ethical Dialogue. Here are individuals who are unwilling to call their core metaphysical beliefs into question but who acknowledge that the application of their beliefs to issues of the world involves a process of learning and modification as they grow in wisdom and experience. They live their lives and practice their faith with the influences of both revelation and reason. They may (quite reasonably) claim that their metaphysical beliefs stemming from revelatory sources enjoy a certain "metaphysical domain privilege" over natural reason, but also recognize that other factors (reason, social situatedness) inevitably inform the way they live their lives, both as believers and in relation to the broader world.[16]

CIVIC VIRTUE: BEYOND PROCEDURALISM

Because the notion of reasonableness—with its animating principles of reciprocity and acceptance of the burdens of judgment—involves evaluative judgments, its effectiveness as a central criterion for political deliberation requires more than a series of procedural steps whose fulfillment can be objectively determined. A strictly proceduralist approach cannot pay adequate heed to our complex, competing visions of the good life. The implications of such proceduralism for schools are bleak: they are forced to move to an increasingly lower common ethical denominator as societal diversity increases, and thus provide an ethical vision that is less and less inspiring to those with richer conceptions.[17] Ethical education, as I have argued, should seek to prepare students for a world in which political questions about the good life are inevitable, and respect compels us to grapple with their ethical diversity; proceduralism, therefore, will not suffice.

In light of this need, a primary goal of ethical education should be to help students (religious and otherwise) recognize both the cost and value of civic virtue: ethical compromises will need to be made in the political realm. This requires students to understand the differences between the private, civic, and political realms as I outlined them at the beginning of chapter 5. Perhaps Callan's caution regarding his alleged "high-wire act" between religious adherence and civic virtue is more treacherous than I acknowledge? "To stay on the wire," Callan asserts, "respect for the limits of the reasonable in our dealings with fellow citizens must be regarded not only as an authentic virtue; it must be prized as a supremely authoritative virtue there because to relax in our respect is to open the door to intolerance toward those who reasonably disagree with us."[18] It is vital to recognize, however, the *context* in which such respect is the supreme virtue— Callan is referring to the political realm, involving instances of state coercion. Reasonableness *should be* the supreme virtue in this context, and to the extent that it conflicts with an individual's religious-ethical framework, the conflict is real and the believer will have to choose between modifying the application of her beliefs to public policy or giving up on civic virtue. But ethical education should also make clear to the believer that giving up on civic virtue imperils all respect for her beliefs as well.

Does it ask too much for religious adherents to make a distinction between the private, civic, and political realms when it comes to applying their ethical frameworks? Many religious adherents in our society understand their religious obligations to include political advocacy of their religiously-informed convictions. As Nicholas Wolterstorff describes it, "Their religion is not, for them, about *something other* than their social and political existence; it is *also* about their social and political existence."[19] Ethical education cannot ignore this reality if the ideals of civic virtue are to be prized and emulated by a wide swath of our society, but neither can the practice of Ethical Dialogue abandon the principles of imaginative engagement and reasonable disagreement, nor the crucial distinctions between the private, civic, and political realms.

Will these liberal distinctions—and their implications for how virtuous citizens may need to modify their arguments and justifications accordingly—ask too much of religious citizens such as Wolterstorff describes? Not necessarily. Wolterstorff's stance on this educational goal as it relates to religious believers strikes me as overly resigned: "Either the religious person almost automatically has secular reasons along with religious reasons for his political positions, or it is going to be very difficult for him to acquire those reasons."[20] One crucial goal of Ethical Dialogue involves striving to enlarge students' conception of reasonableness to include the principles of reciprocity and acceptance of the burdens of judgment. Ethical Dialogue should help them recognize the value and importance of such reasons (which are not strictly secular, despite Wolterstorff's implication) in demonstrating respect toward others, and encourage the practice of giving such reasons during deliberation.

This emphasis on political reasonableness is not the only civic virtue involved in Ethical Dialogue, of course, and the preliminary groundwork of imaginative engagement should serve as an indication to religious students that civic virtue may in fact be more *welcoming* of their private ethical frameworks than they might suspect. An education focused on the civic virtue of Ethical Dialogue should be *at least* as focused on the virtues of a widely inclusive imaginative engagement as it is on delineating the borders of acceptable political argument. To overemphasize the latter is to short-circuit an educational process based on mutual understanding and to needlessly exclude many (often religious) citizens whose respectful participation is vital for the health of our democracy.

But even if religiously fundamentalist students begin to appreciate the civic virtue in distinguishing between deliberation in the private, civic, and political realms, what of their parents? The dangers of an ethical education that is ultimately inhospitable to the ethical-religious frameworks of some parents will likely prompt a blunt question. "While I admit it's possible for my children to retain an unwavering commitment to their faith," a parent might say, "it's also quite possible that an exploration of other ethical frameworks will result in a reduction in their own ethical certainty, perhaps provoking a crisis or even loss of faith. Why should I risk that?" While certainly many religious traditions acknowledge the value of a faith tested and the deepened commitment that can emerge from such a struggle, there are also many religious adherents who seek to shelter themselves and their children from as many such influences as possible. To them, the payoff of a faith strengthened through the challenge of Ethical Dialogue is not worth the risk of apostasy.

So a convincing argument for such an education must take a different tack here: a diverse society in which everyone clings fervently to their private ethical frameworks without acknowledging that many other perspectives deserve tolerance and respect cannot sustain democracy. A refusal to recognize distinctions between private and political realms will in turn threaten all private religious freedom, including that of fundamentalist parents. If I believe I am right and all others who believe differently are unreasonably wrong, then my tolerance—never mind respect—for others' ethical frameworks will extend only as far as their political power will support them. Society becomes a purely political struggle where might equals right and discourse evaporates.

Granted, a few religious adherents will accept this scenario with the faith that their privileged spiritual status will produce political victory, and that "compromise" in the form of mutual understanding is unnecessary and even sinful. An argument for Ethical Dialogue will certainly not sway all religious adherents. But a dialogical education that is sensitive to and inclusive of a variety of ethical frameworks has the potential to nurture a civic realm in which those frameworks are respected far more than at present.

The Ethical Dialogue that teachers model and encourage in their classrooms needs to include a variety of ethical frameworks, including religious. This is important not only to honor the diverse perspectives of students, but because it can add value to ensuing deliberations. Exploring a wider array of perspectives and experiences may contribute to a reduction of bias and a more thoroughly considered judgment. When considering religious perspectives and justifications more specifically, Jeffrey Stout contends that our civic dialogue can benefit when nonadherents can "listen in" on religiously-informed deliberations, by potentially reducing the caricatures of religious believers that do little to promote understanding.[21] While the potential for fostering new insight is compelling, this inclusive approach doesn't prevent the possible tyranny of the majority in political issues, where decision makers may be swayed by an argument—grounded in religious doctrine—with which a minority reasonably disagree. The solution here, of course, cannot be to impose some sort of legal ban on religious reasoning (and other comprehensive ethical frameworks) in political decision making. Drawing the distinction between reasonable and unreasonable justifications would seem to always involve some degree of estimation; in this sense, Ethical Dialogue will continue to rely on a willingness to demonstrate civility, strive for common language, listen thoughtfully, and consider accommodation and compromise. Put simply, we must rely on the exercise of civic virtue, and this in turn depends upon education.

A FINAL PORTRAIT OF CLASSROOM DELIBERATION

To close this chapter on the role of religion in civic deliberation, I will share the second half of the classroom episode I recounted earlier in the chapter. If you recall, the starting point for this discussion had been the question of fate and destiny in *Oedipus Rex*. We had moved from this into a conversation about the role of religion in making laws and policies, and I had observed that disagreement over what counts as evidence makes it difficult to find common ground. At this point I decided to complicate matters a bit, drawing from Deborah Tannen's advice to avoid simple dichotomies—in this case, "religious" and "nonreligious."

"If we disagree on what counts as evidence," I say, "it's going to be tough to find common ground. And keep in mind, using religious reasons doesn't have to be just a problem between religious people and atheists. Believers who argue in support of a graduation prayer often offend people from different faiths."

"How?" Julia asks.

I think back to the many graduation ceremonies I've attended. "Let's say that someone ends a prayer with 'in Jesus' name.' That excludes religions that don't pray in his name."

"Wait a minute," says Julia, clearly getting frustrated. "All these arguments are pushing religion out of society altogether!"

"Well, not completely. People are still free to worship and live religious lives. But it does push for a different kind of reasoning when we decide how to live together." I decide to remind them of the distinctions we've discussed before and sketch them out on the whiteboard. "Remember we've talked about our society having different parts to it—the private, civic, and political? The idea is that we all have private beliefs about the best ways to live, and we bring them into the civic realm to talk about them with each other. But when we make decisions that affect everyone—such as enacting laws and policies—then some people think we ought to base those on reasons we can all share."

"So religious views don't qualify, since they're private and we don't all agree on them?" Claudio asks.

"That's sort of the idea."

Claudio's follow-up comment reveals he is really starting to understand why these issues are so challenging. "There's something not right about this," he finally says. "It sounds like the atheists pretty much get their way. They get laws and policies without religion and force everyone else to go along."

"It's not fair, Mr. Kunzman." Julia understands Claudio's point, and immediately personalizes it. "They act as if religious people can just ignore the things that matter most to us when we decide what society should look like."

"You're both raising good points here. Maybe it asks too much of religious believers for them to find reasons beyond their own religious beliefs." I turn away from where Julia and Claudio are sitting. "What do the rest of you think?"

Sonya goes back to the distinctions I just explained. "What's the big deal? It's not asking religious people to stop believing, it's just saying that you can't drag your own unprovable beliefs into discussions and decisions that affect the rest of us."

I see a bunch of nods affirming Sonya's point, but don't want to miss the opportunity for them to engage imaginatively with what Julia and Claudio are saying. "Well, let's think about how a specific issue might appear to a religious believer under this separation approach." Since I know that Julia and Claudio have their own Christian views in mind, I want to try a different angle to stretch their thinking as well. I draw my example from a newspaper article I saw recently: "Imagine you're a Muslim parent who believes that her children shouldn't be educated in same-sex schools because it is contrary to your moral beliefs informed by your interpretation of Islam. You can't afford private religious school, but all these secular parents and school board members are telling you that your religious reasons don't carry any weight because the decision affects all of them, too, and they don't share your beliefs. They don't have the resources to create a separate school, or even separate classrooms, that would honor your beliefs. How would you feel?"

Sonya replies quickly. "I'd just have to live with it. Majority rules."

"Let's try a little harder here. Don't think about what *you* think the Muslim parent should do; imagine what your perspective would be if your entire way of life was wrapped up in your faith and sticking to a particular moral code. What makes other parents' desires to have coed schools any more justified than your opposition to them? Just because it's the way things have been?"

"This is making my head hurt!"

I smile at that one. "It's tough stuff, but it's important. Especially if you're the one who doesn't get what you want."

Albert keeps trying. "I don't see any way out of this. If the school district can't afford to have both kinds of schools, someone's going to be unhappy and feel like their beliefs are being disrespected."

"That may be true," I admit. "There's no easy answer here, obviously. But it seems important to understand as best we can why people disagree, to try to see it from their perspective, especially when it involves something as personal and important as religion."

Tough-minded Deanna isn't going to let go that easily, though, and I'm glad for that. "Sure, that's nice and all, but we still need some rules about all this, right? What do we do about the Muslim family who wants single-sex schools? I see where they're coming from, but I wouldn't go along with their request."

"OK, let's keep going with this example then." I want to emphasize a key element of Ethical Dialogue here. "Deanna and probably some of the rest of you have reached a point we call 'reasonable disagreement' with this Muslim family. She disagrees—for mostly economic reasons, right?— with their demands for separate schools for boys and girls, but she also sees that it's not unreasonable for them to want to follow religious teachings for their children's education. Have I got the right idea here?"

Deanna nods. "Yes. So what's the fair thing to do?"

My annoyance at forty-five-minute class periods stirs as I notice the clock out of the corner of my eye. "Before the bell rings—anyone want to throw out some ideas we can pick up with tomorrow? Is there any middle ground here we can work toward?" I give my best evil eye to the handful of students who feel compelled to pack up noisily in these waning minutes, and wait for the question to sink in. Finally, wanting to generate at least some closure, I lead them more explicitly: "Where can the district compromise?"

"Could the school do anything to help the Muslim students observe their religious teachings, even if it can't give them everything they want?" Gwen asks.

That strikes me as a good place to start, but to do so we're going to need more information about what specific concerns some Muslims might want addressed besides same-sex classrooms. I consider asking them to do some research on this, but decide that they might have trouble digging this up overnight if they don't know where to look. Instead, I ask them to make a list of the ways in which our school already does accommodate students' special needs, to get them thinking about the potential for flexibility in a diverse society.

The next day, I present students with a list of possible expectations from Muslim parents regarding their children's schooling: no social mixing of sexes; separate classes for gym; no participation in "secular" holidays often celebrated in public schools (e.g., Valentine's Day, Halloween); pork-free food available and labeled in the cafeteria; and accommodations to perform regular religious exercises (brief afternoon prayers and early-excusal on Friday afternoons). I begin by emphasizing that Islam—as with most religions—has great internal diversity, so while this list may apply to some Muslim families, it certainly doesn't apply to all. Then we start to discuss these various accommodations and how they might be implemented. One thing that starts to become clear is that the degree of adjustment on the school's behalf varies widely across the list.

"So in making decisions about what to adjust for these Muslim families, should we just rank the items in order of how much adjustment they require the school to make, then figure out where to draw the line?" I quickly rank them on the board and then say, "Maybe then we would agree to do these first two, part of the third, but not the last two, because they would really force major changes for teachers and everyone else."

What I'm hoping is that we've discussed the significance behind each request enough that someone will see that another factor is at play here. A couple of students have skeptical looks, but no one is speaking up. I try again: "Seems to me we've met them pretty much halfway, agreeing to two-and-a-half of the five requests. Isn't that the ultimate in even compromise?"

Julia—perhaps drawing on insights into her own religious priorities—finally ventures an opinion. "I don't know . . . it seems like some of the little changes schools could make won't be as important to Muslim parents. Something like excusing students for prayer might be a bigger hassle for teachers than avoiding Halloween decorations, but it might mean a lot more to Muslims."

"That a really great point, Julia." I want to emphasize here the importance of understanding before deliberating and deciding. "The more we understand about the values and priorities of Islam, the more we're able to be sensitive to those types of distinctions. We need to weigh what matters most to the school and to individual families and students; some of us may not feel such a sharp clash as the Muslim family we've been imagining, but as citizens we need to take everyone's priorities and needs into consideration."

"I don't get it," Albert says. "A couple days ago, we were talking about how when we're arguing about public policies, it's unfair to use reasons that other people don't accept, like religious teachings. Now you're saying it's OK to use those reasons?"

"Yeah, but just because we take a look at those reasons doesn't mean we have to go by everything they say, right?" Eliza responds. "I mean, it helped us to understand Islamic teachings and the reasons behind them— even if we don't accept all their reasons, it doesn't mean that they don't count for anything."

"But if there aren't any rules for what counts as good reasons," Albert persists, "how are we supposed to know we're making a fair decision?"

"Those are both good points," I say. I don't want to lose everyone else by jumping back into this thorny question of acceptable justifications, so I try to summarize and move us back to concrete details. "We've seen a lot of value in trying to understand the Muslim family's point of view. One thing this makes clear to me is that we have to always be revisiting these types of questions, and keeping the discussion going, even though we might need to make some decisions about how to react now. But Albert's question about consistency is also an important one—do you think we could come up with a list of rules or strategies that we've used in our discussion over the past few days? What has been especially helpful to us as we wrestled with this question?" I start to recap the progression of our discussions, and eventually students start to identify some of the principles involved.

"Trying to see the issue from the perspective of others."

"Figuring out what kinds of reasons everyone can live with, and which ones we disagree about, like religious ones."

"But still letting them be part of the discussion—they might just carry a different amount of weight."

I scribble these and some other, less helpful suggestions on the board; we can narrow the list later. "Great ideas. Let's hear some more . . ."

This classroom episode of Ethical Dialogue ultimately focused on the role of religion in the public square. The central question was not really whether religious perspectives ought to play a role in political deliberation—clearly they do in our American society. Rather, my goal here was to broaden my students' understanding of the challenges that such a reality brings with it, and to engage imaginatively with the various attitudes toward religion in the American public square. Then, by shifting to the specific topic of public schooling and Islamic beliefs, I challenged students to devise and defend reasonable "ground rules" for such political interactions. An effective attempt at this comes only after a thoughtful and ongoing process of clarification and empathetic engagement.[22]

As I continue to emphasize throughout this book, Ethical Dialogue is not asking students to "do philosophy" in any formal sense of the phrase. The terms *reciprocity* and *acceptance of the burdens of judgment* never arose in this classroom discussion, nor did they at other points during the school year. This is first-order ethical reflection and deliberation. Furthermore, Ethical Dialogue does not focus on a series of procedural rules. The goal is to develop students' appreciation for the requirements of civic virtue, and the need for compromise it often entails. The compromises and conclusions to such deliberation need not be definitive; Ethical Dialogue in classrooms is much more about learning skills and virtues than drawing political conclusions, about experiencing a cultivation of shared norms and a commitment to mutual edification rather than manipulation. The norms of political community rest on a willingness to make civic virtue a penultimate commitment of sorts. While people will undeniably live the bulk of their lives in the nonpolitical realms guided by their private visions of the good life, mutual respect requires a different sort of commitment when we decide how we will live *together*.

The focus of these last two chapters has been on civically virtuous political deliberation. The cultivation of this civic virtue, with its emphasis on mutual goodwill and the acceptance of reasonable disagreement, is a continual and vital process. Because the political realm is under constant negotiation, our efforts toward imaginative engagement must continue as well. While in some ways the process of political deliberation requires more complicated regulation than (private and civic) dialogue not involving state power, its lengthy treatment in this chapter should not be taken as an indication of its relative emphasis in Ethical Dialogue. As I stressed in the preceding section on civic virtue, laying the groundwork of imaginative engagement is at least as important. Without thoughtful efforts toward understanding unfamiliar ethical frameworks, any ensuing political deliberation will suffer from a lack of respect and—more likely than not—a conclusion determined more by social power than our capacity to reason together.

7

Preparing Teachers
for Ethical Dialogue

I have emphasized repeatedly in these pages that Ethical Dialogue is within the reach of most students. While the goal of imaginative engagement and the principles of reasonableness (reciprocity and acceptance of the burdens of judgment) are vital concepts, students do not need a philosophical understanding of them in order to engage in Ethical Dialogue. Students can seek empathetic understanding and appreciate the existence of reasonable disagreement and its implications for making decisions together in society, all without ever hearing the technical terms I have presented. (In the same way, most students appreciate curricula that employ a variety of media and learning formats, but have never heard of "multimodal instruction" or even "multiple intelligences.")

But what about teachers? What degree of second-order understanding is necessary for them to be effective facilitators of Ethical Dialogue, and to what extent is such insight attainable by most of the teaching force? This latter question includes consideration not only of teachers' conceptual understanding and pedagogical skills, but also their sense of the purposes of teaching and the environmental constraints that surround their work. The aim of this chapter is to consider the implications of Ethical Dialogue for professional development broadly construed. My intent is not to provide a detailed blueprint for policy or teacher education but to make a preliminary case that—while challenging—preparing teachers to facilitate Ethical Dialogue is a realistic and achievable goal.

I frame this task as involving three essential elements: capacity, commitment, and collaboration. Teachers need to develop the *capacity* for Ethical Dialogue, including basic conceptual understandings as well as a range of facilitation skills. Just as important as this capacity is a *commitment* by teachers and administrators acknowledging the vital importance of Ethical Dialogue for both students' education and the health of our democracy. Neither capacity nor commitment will be adequately achieved, however, without a spirit and practice of *collaboration* among these stakeholders.

Before addressing each of these in detail, I want to emphasize an overarching principle for teacher preparation. If Ethical Dialogue (or any other substantive reforms, for that matter) is to take root in our schools, then the typical conception of "teacher education" must expand. We must view teacher education from a developmental standpoint: the myriad skills and knowledge that a quality teacher needs cannot possibly be mastered in a one-year graduate program, much less as part of a four-year undergraduate experience. The implications here of "teacher as lifelong learner" for ongoing professional development are substantial: it cannot be seen as a secondary feature of a teacher's experience, a periodic "fine-tuning" of already mastered skills and dispositions.

Preservice teacher education generally involves novices who are (understandably) much more focused on teaching methods related to classroom management and familiarity with disciplinary subject matter. Most teacher educators are familiar with the question from student teachers, "How does this help me when I teach my class *tomorrow?*" Preservice educators certainly need to be cognizant of that felt need among novices, but they should also seek to instill in prospective teachers a *vision* of teaching that may extend beyond their current capacity to implement it, a vision that places great importance on helping students learn to engage respectfully with ethical diversity. Researchers who examine the effectiveness of multicultural teacher education—of which ethical diversity should certainly be a part—recognize that novice teachers cannot possibly master all of the knowledge and skills required for culturally responsive teaching, but they *can* develop a vision for what it entails and how it can be accomplished. This vision helps provide the impetus necessary for continued growth beyond their initial preparation, although this must be supported by long-term professional opportunities for ongoing critical reflection and collaboration.[1]

TEACHER CAPACITY FOR ETHICAL DIALOGUE

Teachers need to develop both a conceptual understanding of the principles embedded in Ethical Dialogue as well as pedagogical skill in guiding students through a process of imaginative engagement and civic deliberation. In addition, teachers need to appreciate the importance of pedagogical even-handedness and church-state separation. (Perhaps this is obvious, but teachers also need to be informed citizens themselves—reading newspapers, seeking out varied perspectives, and considering where they stand on issues being discussed in the public square.) As with any form of pedagogical content knowledge, the biggest challenge is not mastering content alone or mastering facilitation skills alone, but learning how to best facilitate dialogue involving that content.[2]

Let me be clear that by conceptual understanding, I do not mean to imply that teachers need extensive, detailed training in philosophical ethics or religious studies. Part of the expectation here is that teachers will be familiar with general principles—legal and theoretical—surrounding Ethical Dialogue. Their level of understanding of the foundational principles of Ethical Dialogue will need to be more substantial than that of their students, but the emphasis here is on educational *concepts* rather than philosophical *terminology*. Just as with students, technical terms such as reciprocity and burdens of judgment need not be part of teachers' vocabulary (again, we might consider a parallel example: I have observed many student teachers who make it a point to capture their students' interest at the beginning of class, without ever having heard the term "anticipatory set").

Teachers *will* need to develop a clear sense of how Ethical Dialogue contributes to broader educational ends, however, and particularly why student reflection and thoughtfulness are vital dispositions to be cultivated. In addition, one strand of specific terminology with which teachers should be familiar is the set of distinctions between the private, civic, and political realms. I have argued for the importance of cultivating shared reasons in the political realm, but this tripartite distinction matters just as much in another, more inclusive sense. This book sets itself apart from much standard liberal political theory in emphasizing the ample civic space outside of the political realm, where efforts toward imaginative engagement cultivate the morally vital groundwork for necessary political deliberation. The more that teachers can help their students appreciate these distinctions, the more students will feel that their private ethical frameworks are acknowledged and considered in the civic realm. This perception, I believe, will contribute to a greater appreciation among students-as-citizens that civic and political deliberation are vital endeavors in promoting mutual respect and social justice.

Many teachers will also need a clearer understanding of key boundaries regarding pedagogical neutrality and, in particular, separation of church and state issues. On the latter point, I have already acknowledged that public school teachers are understandably wary of violating church-state boundaries. Certainly this concern is an important one. Historian of education David Tyack tells the story of a workshop he once led for public school social studies teachers exploring how the study of religion could be thoughtfully included in their curricula. At the end of their week together, one enthusiastic participant approached him and exclaimed, "Professor Tyack, I just want to thank you for helping me to figure out how I can go back and lead all my students to Jesus!" Needless to say, this was neither Tyack's intention nor his message, but it seems the teacher had filtered the workshop's objectives through a particularly evangelistic framework.[3]

Nel Noddings likely had this type of phenomenon in mind when she made the clearly valid point that "it can be very hard for teachers with strong religious commitments to maintain religious neutrality." But this claim overlooks a broader consideration. The challenge of neutrality certainly applies to atheists as well, many of whom have strong feelings about religion. And while many scholars point to the tendency of Protestants to overemphasize the importance of belief and doctrine in studying religion, the broader Western analytical tradition also places a premium on identifying underlying principles and the importance of written texts. The potential for biases can be found in many forms. What is important to recognize here, however, is that civic virtue cannot be realized by *ignoring* religion any more than it can by adopting the perspective of Tyack's workshop student.[4]

What seems clear is the need for greater confidence on the part of teachers regarding legal policy for exploration of religious issues. The large majority of teachers are not familiar with current guidelines, and their ignorance generally results in a blanket avoidance of religious topics, particularly when involving more than rote facts.[5] Tyack's story notwithstanding, I find that most teachers need to be assured that they have *more* latitude for exploration of religion and ethics than they assume, not less.

Teacher neutrality is not embodied through an *avoidance* of ethical issues; in fact, this may send the decidedly *non*-neutral message that the societal status quo is perfectly acceptable.

As I discussed earlier, learning to teach is an ongoing endeavor that ideally stretches over the course of a career. Without a core set of skills for inquiry and analysis, teachers will have great difficulty continuing the developmental process necessary to master the complexities of quality teaching. One foundational skill necessary for this challenge, Robert Floden asserts, is "knowledge about inquiry. To guide classroom discussions so that they lead to justified conclusions, teachers need to understand criteria for evaluating arguments and conjectures."[6] Teachers need to become skilled at framing issues clearly and developing thoughtful questions; connecting previous knowledge with new learning; clarifying, summarizing, and building upon student responses; fostering an environment in which students engage directly with one another; and encouraging the habit of careful listening and charitable interpretation of opposing arguments. In this sense, the actual pedagogical skills necessary for facilitation of Ethical Dialogue share many similarities with those necessary for leading any effective, open-ended discussion and should be an ongoing focus for all teachers seeking to engage their students in all kinds of active learning.

PROFESSIONAL COMMITMENT TO ETHICAL DIALOGUE

Because the demands of Ethical Dialogue are substantial—in terms of curricular attention, pedagogical complexity, and emotional weight—it cannot be sustained unless teachers (and the administrators who support them) are convinced of its vital importance. In particular, teachers need to recognize that the health of our increasingly pluralistic society depends on people who can deliberate respectfully across difference.

As I mentioned earlier, research demonstrates the limited role that preservice education can play in preparing teachers for the complexity of Ethical Dialogue and other facets of multicultural education. This same research, however, stresses the importance of cultivating a commitment and vision of what is possible as teachers grow in their profession. While some preservice programs have made significant efforts in this direction, they are rare.[7] In the preservice methods classes that I teach, one of the pedagogical issues we discuss is what to do when controversial issues arise in the classroom. When I ask students to compose a short position paper in response to our discussion, they reveal a range of thinking. Most of them do believe that they should encourage certain moral values (interpersonal obligations), and some also see broader ethical questions of meaning and purpose as important for students to consider. The responses that specifically address the role of religion almost invariably acknowledge that they should not impose their own beliefs, but some are far more cautious. "I certainly don't want to step on the toes of particular denominations and sects or the principal and school board," one future teacher wrote. "This topic will strictly be student-based discussion, if I allow it at all."

Others express the mistaken view that it is simply illegal to discuss religion in public schools. Even though the type of exploration I advocate in this book is constitutionally permissible, why should teachers and schools risk wading into these murky waters of ethics, politics, and religion? As I've pointed out, they already stand knee-deep; questions about the good life and how to live together amidst ethical disagreement are already present in schools and curricula. The question is whether to acknowledge and engage with them, or ignore or even prohibit their consideration. One prospective teacher shared his mixed feelings here; he recognized the importance of ethical and religious issues in the lives of his students and society, but confessed, "Dealing with religion in the classroom really terrifies me, because I am afraid of making students uncomfortable and also the consequences of having a religious discussion in my classroom."

We should not dismiss these concerns lightly, of course. While I hope to have provided a vision for how such conversations can occur, I realize that by its very nature, Ethical Dialogue frequently involves issues of deep complexity and great importance to students and teachers alike. In her research on classroom discussion of controversial public issues, Diana Hess suggests several reasons why teachers do not engage students in such discussion, including time constraints, concerns about maintaining classroom control, and the challenges of facilitating dialogue about complex issues. As Natasha Levinson observes, teachers often decide to avoid such dialogue altogether: "Sometimes they do this in the name of moral neutrality that is borne either out of legalistic fears of crossing the line separating church and state, or out of pedagogical concerns that their position of authority may unduly influence the direction of their students' moral development. At other times, they simply want to avoid conflict in their classrooms, since conflict is not only uncomfortable but noisy. It can also appear to be unproductive."[8]

In addition, larger roadblocks loom beyond the classroom walls. In his classic 1975 study, Dan Lortie emphasized that teachers work within *structures* that frequently limit their capacity to change; this situation seems to have improved little since then.[9] While I have made it a point from the outset of this book to specify that my focus is limited to the classroom level of practice rather than broader school or community elements, I certainly acknowledge the impact that these broader structures have on classroom practice, particularly now in the age of standards-based testing. At the same time, however, many teachers exercise a significant degree of autonomy in terms of *how* they address curricular standards; the key for an approach such as Ethical Dialogue, it seems, is to find ways to merge content and dialogue in a synergistic whole.

As I acknowledged previously, curricular "coverage" will likely have to be sacrificed somewhat if Ethical Dialogue is to have substantial focus and depth, a decision that is also very likely made beyond the classroom walls. But I would also contend that Ethical Dialogue will generally be most effective when embedded in regular subject matter, not as a separate add-on that is not seen as central to the academic focus of the classroom. By weaving ethical exploration within existing curricula, teachers can do "double duty" to some extent, achieving multiple learning outcomes concurrently. I have found that the relationship between *engaging in* Ethical Dialogue and a *commitment to* Ethical Dialogue is a mutually encouraging one; teachers who explore such issues in their classes will likely come to appreciate more fully their importance and value (and student engagement with them), thus strengthening their commitment to further Ethical Dialogue, and so on.

Both elements—capacity and commitment—are necessary for teachers to effectively foster Ethical Dialogue. Obviously, even a teacher who has the requisite knowledge and skills, but who sees ethical education as outside his purview, will find little use for Ethical Dialogue. But the opposite is certainly true as well, as it takes more than good intentions to engage students in complex ethical issues in ways that are developmentally appropriate. In a qualitative study of teaching culturally diverse students, for example, Gretchen McAllister writes of the danger of a "false sense of involvement" and the "paradox of appropriation" that occur when teachers' empathy is not bolstered by technical competence and subject matter knowledge.[10] Teacher capacity *and* commitment are essential, but neither are likely to develop sufficiently unless educators are provided ongoing, collaborative opportunities for professional development.

COLLABORATION AS CENTRAL
TO PROFESSIONAL DEVELOPMENT

Most teachers I know are not fans of in-service days. They typically see these as time-consuming impositions with little relevance to their actual practice or specific needs as a professional. The gap between typical in-service foci and the improvement of teacher practice is obviously problematic. But even teacher development opportunities that deal directly with pedagogy cannot consist of disconnected, one-day workshops if they seek to bring about substantive, lasting change. A committed process of focused attention is necessary for an approach such as Ethical Dialogue to become successful.

Helping teachers become adept at fostering Ethical Dialogue also requires a strong emphasis on peer collaboration. Working with colleagues can offer interdisciplinary insights, expose teachers to a wider array of ethical frameworks, and provide opportunities for constructive critique of their pedagogy. Perhaps most importantly, peer collaboration offers teachers the chance to connect on a philosophical level with others, to develop a joint vision for ethical education that provides the encouragement necessary to persevere in spite of its ample challenges.

In many of the graduate courses I teach, I am fortunate to have former or current public school teachers who help us consider in authentic detail the omnipresent gap between theory and practice. One day during a seminar focused on Ethical Dialogue, three former math teachers happened to embark on a passionate and argumentative tangent about the most effective strategies for teaching math. I think the rest of us were somewhat impressed with the near ferocity that these otherwise mild-mannered colleagues brought to the topic. Finally one of them turned to me and remarked, "If teachers like us feel so strongly about a subject like math, imagine the controversies that erupt over religion in the classroom!" On the one hand, this comment might be seen as good reason to avoid talking with colleagues about Ethical Dialogue. The work will not be easy, nor always comfortable. But it is this experience of grappling that teachers need if they are to help their students do the same. The collaborative process of making our ethical perspectives intelligible to one another is practice for Ethical Dialogue itself, as well as an important step in creating a wider school culture that communicates to students that ethical exploration is worth their attention.

The value of collaboration in preparing teachers for Ethical Dialogue should not be underestimated. Research suggests that professional development featuring peer coaching and collaborative inquiry between teachers can effectively influence their pedagogy and—even more significantly—their deeply held beliefs about student learning. Effective professional development provides opportunities for supportive yet challenging conversations about teaching. It provides the time for colleagues to analyze pedagogical challenges, the safety to admit uncertainties and seek advice from others, and the chance to examine artifacts of classroom practice (student work, lesson plans, etc.). In particular, professional development aimed at Ethical Dialogue needs to emphasize the importance of scaffolding teachers' understanding and seeking a process of gradual change. Schools and teachers must make a substantial, ongoing commitment to cultivating these skills and dispositions in themselves and their students.[11]

In my view, perhaps the most valuable benefit of teacher collaboration is the opportunity it can provide educators to discuss and consider their central beliefs about the purposes of schooling, particularly as they regard ethical exploration. Research on teachers' professional lives has found that many feel interpersonally and philosophically disconnected from their colleagues. Given that teachers are resistant to changes that are incongruent with their personal beliefs about teaching, conducting conversations around these deeper normative commitments seems vital if school communities are going to embrace substantive reform such as Ethical Dialogue. Furthermore, many ethical questions inevitably cross disciplines, such as those involving the use of technology (often requiring consideration of physics, biology, economics, government, etc.). Since teachers cannot possibly develop an extensive knowledge base in so many areas, the opportunity to talk with and learn from colleagues can provide them with important insights from unfamiliar disciplines.[12]

At the conclusion of chapter 4, I referred to Katherine Simon's recent book that advocated the classroom exploration of ethical questions. One particular strength of Simon's approach is her heavy emphasis on teacher collaboration. She suggests that schools provide forums for teachers to consider the ethical implications of their curricula, and proposes the use of "critical friends" to visit teachers' classrooms and provide constructive feedback on pedagogy. "The program I suggest is not a project for individual teachers," Simon advises, "It absolutely depends on groups of teachers working together to support and complement one another within a context that nurtures this work."[13]

As I explained in chapter 5, teachers have an obligation to present all legitimate sides of an ethical issue as fairly and fully as possible. This approach, which helps fulfill the principle of reciprocity, has important implications for collaborative teacher development as well. In particular, this can help increase teachers' awareness of their own social locations—both the understanding they provide and the limits they impose—as crucial preparation for dealing with diversity in the classroom. Collaborating with other teachers who inhabit diverse social locations can provide helpful insight into ethical frameworks that are inaccessible from their own first-person perspective. The more teachers can talk with colleagues about topics for Ethical Dialogue, the more they can be helped to recognize the implications of their curricular and pedagogical choices; such collaborative efforts may help guard against their own individual ethical frameworks inappropriately dominating their work with students. As part of this collegial approach, Simon argues that teachers should have the opportunity to jointly examine and discuss student work on ethical issues and to conduct reciprocal peer observations. She acknowledges that these techniques are certainly not foolproof but contends that "such a system—by openly acknowledging the importance of addressing complex issues honestly and thoroughly—would be a significant improvement over the status quo, in which teachers may impoverish the curriculum by trying to avoid all controversy or may simply give students their own, unchallenged version of the truth."[14]

While not professional development aimed specifically at Ethical Dialogue, the following examples of teacher collaboration share many similar educational goals. My goal in providing these brief snapshots is not to "prove" that these efforts "work" as much as to illustrate some ways that schools and districts are providing opportunities for teachers to discuss ethical issues and how they might address them in their classrooms.

At Thomas Jefferson High School for Science and Technology in northern Virginia, ongoing professional development was designed that sought to make ethical questions more central in its public school curriculum. Teachers obtained funding from the National Endowment for the Humanities to develop a three-week summer program and seven one-day follow-up sessions during the next school year. Through the discussion of literature and other texts, teachers addressed questions such as: "What is a good life?"; "What is a good society?"; and "What should the relationship be between the individual and society, and between communities and the state?" Teachers also discussed how they could incorporate these questions effectively into their various curricula, and the follow-up sessions offered opportunities to reflect on how those efforts were going and provide suggestions and encouragement for their colleagues.[15]

With the phrase "Living with Our Deepest Differences" as its central motif, the San Bernardino, California, school system sponsored in-service workshops that considered how to address various religious traditions in the curriculum in ways that emphasized understanding and respectful engagement. Also included were discussions about how to respond to student needs surrounding diet, prayer, and interpersonal interactions (e.g., recognizing certain social restrictions for conservative Muslim students). Teachers worked directly with constitutional experts and religious studies scholars from local universities to better understand how to explore religion sensitively, both legally and culturally. The district also offered a "Teacher as Researcher" opportunity for interested faculty, who engaged in a systematic evaluation of their own classroom efforts.[16]

Schools or districts that implement clear and thoughtful policies regarding efforts toward Ethical Dialogue can also assist teachers. During the early 1990s, the Williamsville Central School District in western New York garnered national attention for controversy surrounding the broader school curriculum during religious holidays (including assemblies and use of symbols), particularly at Christmastime. One noteworthy outgrowth of this episode was the creation of district policies to provide educators with guidance on the teaching of religion, sensitivity to student concerns such as dietary restrictions, and the development of staff resources (e.g., informational texts) and regular in-service requirements aimed at teacher dialogue surrounding religious and ethical issues. When done with sensitivity and a nuanced understanding of various traditions, such guidelines can provide additional counsel and reassurance to teachers as they encourage Ethical Dialogue in their classrooms.[17]

Through her teacher development efforts at the Coalition of Essential Schools, Katherine Simon conducts the "Essential Moral Questions Summer Institute." This week-long gathering of K–12 teachers addresses such questions as: What would it look like if students were discussing Essential Moral Questions in depth? How does it feel to us to discuss heated, morally charged issues with our peers? What works in facilitating such a conversation? What is scary about addressing EMQs? How should my passionately held political or moral beliefs influence my work as teacher? What type of scaffolding is necessary to promote student understanding? Are there topics that should be off limits in the classroom? Here again Simon emphasizes the importance of peer collaboration: participants join the Institute in teams from their local schools. This also helps avoid the pitfalls of disconnected, "one-shot-deal" professional development experiences: teachers return to their schools with a team vision and a supportive context in which to continue their professional growth. In a follow-up interview, one participant credited the EMQ Institute with "reinforcing the idea of questions and the importance of asking complex questions that we might not necessarily all agree on." In addition, it helped create "a culture in the classroom where we can ask questions like that respectfully, and . . . [where we can] rely on each other to conduct that kind of inquiry responsibly and thoughtfully."[18]

Preparing teachers for Ethical Dialogue is a challenging proposition, and my goal in this chapter has not been to downplay its complexity. But if we believe that preparing students to engage respectfully with the increasing ethical diversity of American society is a vital element of a healthy democracy, then we should not be too quick to deem it out of reach. Rather, we should look to examples such as those cited above—not necessarily for total replication, but certainly for inspiration—and keep in mind that while significant curricular changes are obviously daunting, they are not unheard of. Think, for instance, of the ongoing inclusion of women and ethnic minorities in the curriculum. Broader changes to school structure and pedagogy are perhaps even more difficult, but consider the shift in special education toward a policy of inclusion and mainstreaming that has occurred in recent years—this, too, might have been thought impossible before it actually began to happen. Teachers vary widely in their capacities and commitments, but we would do well not to underestimate them, nor the students whom they teach, as we seek to foster deeper understanding and respectful engagement across ethical difference.

8

Conclusion

"One of the greatest normative problems with which we must deal is the existence of deep and apparently irresolvable moral disagreements," David Wong observes. "We must know how to act when no single side in a disagreement can show that it has the best arguments." The increasing diversity of our society shouldn't lead us to shy away from in-depth exploration of and deliberation about our ethical frameworks. Rather, the need to engage and respect this diversity *demands* that our schools prepare citizens to do this. My core philosophical argument in these pages has been that—particularly in the context of deep ethical conflict—respect requires that we understand the ethical frameworks of others. But to expect this respectful engagement by citizens who have not had the opportunity to develop the skills and virtues of Ethical Dialogue in the public educational realm seems unrealistic. As Michael Walzer observes, "Democracy is still, always, a politics of strain. . . . That is why education is so important—school learning (also practical experience) aimed at producing the patience, stamina, tolerance, and receptiveness without which the strain will not be understood or accepted." Helping students incorporate religion into the civic conversation is a daunting challenge, but one worth the strain.[1]

I began this book by contending that the history of ethical education in the United States prior to the 1960s was a legal, political, and moral failure. The shift away from a singular ethical model in response was understandable and justified, but the "solutions" that took shape in the form of values clarification, cognitive-developmental theory, and now character education have also failed to serve the needs of an ethically diverse society. The attempt to address ethical issues in abstraction from deeper ethical sources has left us hamstrung in our capacity to engage thoughtfully across the issues—moral, religious, cultural—that often divide us.

The role of religion in many ethical frameworks is undeniably substantial and thus has received particular attention in this book. Our often lamentable history of Protestant hegemony has never completely disappeared, and many would argue that it has retained significant influence even in our public schools. Nevertheless, ignoring religion or approaching it with complete academic detachment will not foster the type of empathic understanding that I contend is crucial if we are to respect our fellow citizens and deliberate thoughtfully about how to live together amidst our differences.

Clearly, this is challenging work and requires substantial commitment by schools and teachers. What Ethical Dialogue is *not*, however, is esoteric. I have emphasized throughout this book that Ethical Dialogue does not require students to act as philosophers in any formal sense, complete with understanding of technical terms and highly structured analytical arguments. Rather, Ethical Dialogue is more accurately understood as a process of *grappling*, a term I have borrowed from Ted and Nancy Sizer. "Circling back over familiar ground, asking new sorts of questions about that ground, and looking for every scrap of data are necessary steps in building the habit of thoughtful grappling," they write. "A student who grapples is made aware of this complexity. And if there is an explicit assumption on the part of the school and its teachers that this sort of grappling is as worthy as it is complex, the student may get into the habit of the struggle."[2] Such grappling within and among students is the heart of Ethical Dialogue.

The Sizers' reference here to the broader school community should not be overlooked. As I explained in chapter 1, this book focuses on classroom-level curricula; nevertheless, I fully acknowledge the importance of what occurs outside the classroom door in reinforcing the skills and commitments of Ethical Dialogue. Certainly much recent research bears this out.[3] Schools that model a broad commitment to Ethical Dialogue will undoubtedly support classroom learning, but even more important is the foundational attitude of respect that people demonstrate to one another. If schools promote Ethical Dialogue as part of the formal curricula but offer no support or encouragement for students (and adults) to similarly address ethical differences in the hallways, playgrounds, and lunchrooms, it seems highly unlikely that students will develop any lasting commitment to such a process.

Another legitimate question involving the setting for Ethical Dialogue might focus on whether schools are the best context for such an education to occur. Why not other social institutions, both civic and private? What role might entities such as political organizations, news media, religious groups, and others play in creating opportunities for Ethical Dialogue? My response here is that, as I suggested in the opening chapter, schools should *not* be the only venues for such ethical education; their efforts will almost certainly prove insufficient if not echoed and amplified in broader society. Perhaps schools are not even the *best* setting, given the multitude of educational responsibilities they currently bear. Nevertheless, few social institutions seem currently inclined or positioned to cultivate Ethical Dialogue in our citizenry in any comprehensive sense, and many have their own set of limitations (news media rarely foster actual substantive dialogue among citizens, for example, preferring to deal in sound bites or "expert discussants"). And even if legitimate postschooling venues were to emerge, it seems far more likely that citizens will be inclined and equipped to participate in those opportunities if their school years were spent developing the skills and dispositions necessary for respectful involvement. Schools are an important venue for developing a commitment to the civic virtue enacted through Ethical Dialogue.

The still-elusive holy grail of moral and character education has been producing not only students who exhibit superior moral reasoning, but people who actually act on this in their lives. Unfortunately, most research points to a low correlation between moral cognition and behavior; just because students gain a better appreciation of morally appropriate behavior, this seems to have little impact on whether they embody it in their lives. In terms of more specific citizenship virtues, a literature review of social studies curricula found that they also had little effect on students' civic commitments, either in terms of attitudes or behaviors.[4]

Similarly, it is worth acknowledging that a commitment to Ethical Dialogue does not guarantee the creation of better, more moral citizens. At the same time, however, it is difficult to imagine how—in our ethically diverse American society—such citizens could exist without demonstrating a commitment to respectful engagement with those differing perspectives. The debate between inculcating moral virtue and fostering broader ethical reflectiveness is unnecessarily dichotomized; effective citizenship depends on the interplay between the two capacities. As Damon and Colby observe in their work on the relationship between education and moral commitment, "The heart of moral growth is not simply acquiring good habits *or* insightful reflectiveness; rather, it is developing the capacity to move easily between the two."[5] While Ethical Dialogue focuses on developing the capacity for insightful reflectiveness, it also depends on moral commitments to mutual respect and reciprocity.

Liberal democracy relies on the distinction between the private and the civic. In this book, I have sought to preserve this vital distinction while arguing that greater attention needs to be paid to fostering a substantive appreciation for the diverse, private ethical frameworks in our society as a precursor to deliberation. Both imaginative engagement and ensuing civic deliberation deserve far greater curricular attention in our public schools. Students, in developing their capacities as citizens, need to learn about more than the political history and governmental structures found on standardized exams. The civic and political realms have necessary and important boundaries, but must be informed by the private realm's deep ethical frameworks if they are to have any purchase and power in our lives together.

There is currently little room for public school students to explore these diverse ethical frameworks—except in the thin Heroes and Holidays sense—and even less for thoughtful deliberation in the face of ethical conflict. Even while advocating a strict notion of public reason, Eamonn Callan criticizes liberals' lack of clarity about how to help students engage with ethical diversity. "Were that clarity available," he contends, "we might find that we liberals have much more in common with many who cherish faith and tradition than we ever thought we had."[6] My goal in these pages has been to present a clearer vision of such engagement in the hope that my readers will recognize that a liberal education can both accommodate and be strengthened by grappling with the good, with the deep ethical sources that guide our private lives and inevitably inform our civic perspectives as well.

I concluded chapter 7 with the contention that while substantive educational reform can be extraordinarily challenging, it is a challenge worth meeting. "We cannot in good educational conscience avoid the serious and volatile disputes on religious and moral matters because they are controversial, complex, and outrageously perplexing," contends David Purpel. "Quite the contrary: *because* they are so important and *since* they beg for awareness, understanding, clarification, and insight, they are central to significant educational inquiry."[7] How we respond to these challenges will say a great deal about what we see as the purposes of public education. To the extent that we believe in the importance of learning how to be a public, how to live together in respect and understanding, then such a commitment is worth making.

Notes

CHAPTER 1

1. Throughout this book, I provide a variety of classroom examples and vignettes, all of which are drawn from my own teaching or my observations of other classrooms. In some cases, I have compressed the time frame and dialogue; other times, I present episodes that are composites of multiple experiences. My purpose in sharing them is to illustrate the challenges and potential of such curricula, not provide a literal qualitative snapshot.

2. Bernard Williams, *Ethics and the Limits of Philosophy* (Cambridge, MA: Harvard University Press, 1985).

3. Lawrence J. Walker, "Moral Exemplarity" in *Bringing in a New Era in Character Education*, ed. William Damon, 65, 66 (Stanford, CA: Hoover Institution Press, 2002); William Damon and Anne Gregory, "The Youth Charter: Towards the Formation of Adolescent Moral Identity," *Journal of Moral Education* 26, no. 2 (1997): 117–30; Daniel K. Lapsley, "Pluralism, Virtues, and the Post-Kohlbergian Era in Moral Psychology," in *The Challenge of Pluralism: Education, Politics, and Values*, ed. F. Clark Power and Daniel Lapsley, 169–99 (Notre Dame, IN: University of Notre Dame Press, 1992).

4. Patrik Jonsson, "Edgy First College Assignment: Study the Koran," *Christian Science Monitor*, July 30, 2002, sec. 3, p. 1.

5. Katherine G. Simon, *Moral Questions in the Classroom: How to Get Kids to Think Deeply about Real Life and Their Schoolwork* (New Haven, CT: Yale University Press, 2001), 53–54.

6. James S. Leming, "Reflections on Thirty Years of Moral Education Research," *Moral Education Forum* 20 (1995): 6; Institutes and curricular programs devoted to ethical education number in the thousands. Barely a month into his inaugural year of 2001, President George W. Bush pledged to triple federal funding for character education. At that time, at least forty states were already involved in character education efforts through legislative mandates or federal grants (see Charles C. Haynes and Oliver Thomas, *Finding Common Ground: A Guide to Religious Liberty in Public Schools* (Nashville, TN: First Amendment Center, 2001), 159).

7. Michelle Fine et al., "Civics Lessons: The Color and Class of Betrayal," *Teachers College Record* 106, no. 11 (2004): 2193–2223; Daniel Solomon et al., "Creating Classrooms That Students Experience As Communities," *American Journal of Community Psy-*

chology 24, no. 6 (1996): 719–48; Daniel Solomon, Marilyn S. Watson, and Victor A. Battistich, "Teaching and Schooling Effects on Moral/Prosocial Development," in *Handbook of Research on Teaching*, 4th ed., ed. Virginia Richardson, 566–603 (Washington, DC: American Educational Research Association, 2001); Victor Battistich et al., "Caring School Communities," *Educational Psychologist* 32, no. 3 (1997): 137–51; James S. Leming, "Character Education and the Creation of Community," *The Responsive Community* 4, no. 4 (1994): 49–57.

8. Richard G. Niemi and Jane Junn, *Civic Education: What Makes Students Learn* (New Haven, CT: Yale University Press, 1998); James Youniss, Jeffrey A. McClellan, and Miranda Yates, "What We Know about Engendering Civic Identity," *American Behavioral Scientist* 40, no. 5 (1997): 625; see also Miranda Yates and James Youniss, "A Developmental Perspective on Community Service in Adolescence," *Social Development* 5, no. 1 (1996): 85–109.

9. David E. Purpel, *The Moral and Spiritual Crisis in Education: A Curriculum for Justice and Compassion in Education* (South Hadley, MA: Bergin and Garvey, 1989), 68.

Chapter 2

1. *Roemer v. Maryland Public Works Board*, 426 US 736 (1976), 745–46.

2. Bess Keller, "Dalai Lama's 'Summit' Stirs Debate for Schools," *Education Week* 20, no. 37 (May 23, 2001): 3.

3. Randal C. Archibold, "School District Is Cleared in Lawsuit over Religion," *New York Times*, March 29, 2001, p. B6.

4. Caroline Hendrie, "Mich. District Ordered to Pay Fees for Girl in 'Diversity Week' Case," *Education Week* 24, no. 8 (October 20, 2004): 4.

5. *Hood v. Medford Township Board of Education*, 533 US 915 (2001); George F. Will, "Protect Religious Speech, Too," *San Jose Mercury News*, February 27, 2001, p. 7C.

6. Jonathan Zimmerman, *Whose America?: Culture Wars in the Public Schools* (Cambridge, MA: Harvard University Press, 2002), 7–8; James W. Fraser, *Between Church and State: Religion and Public Education in a Multicultural America* (New York: St. Martin's Press, 1999), 4.

7. Admittedly, the disjunction between the realm of federal educational policy and the practices of locally controlled districts creates a historiographical challenge. We have far less certainty about the latter area, but that ambiguity does not significantly interfere with my purpose here, which is to describe how the broader cultural and political shifts have brought us to the current state of educational practice in schools. In addition, it is important to acknowledge that the history of education in what would become the United States includes far more than the British colonies and their progeny, and writing history from the primary vantage point of the "victors" is often problematic and misleadingly incomplete. But while other regions and peoples—American Indians, for example—certainly figure into the larger story of ethical education, the perspectives and influences of the European settlers set the tone for church-state issues which unfolded in American history.

8. Thomas Jefferson to Danbury Baptist Association, quoted in H. A. Washington, ed., *The Writings of Thomas Jefferson*, ed. H. A. Washington, VII: 113 (Washington, DC: Taylor and Maury, 1854); quote cited in R. Freeman Butts, *The American Tradition in Religion and Education* (Boston: Beacon Press, 1950), 92–93; Butts cites evidence that, contrary to interpretations that depict Jefferson's metaphor as part of an insubstantial courtesy letter, Jefferson took great care in his wording to the point of seeking legal advice (pp. 93–94).

9. B. Edward McClellan, *Moral Education in America: Schools and the Shaping of Character from Colonial Times to the Present* (New York: Teachers College Press, 1999), 13; Provisions were made soon after the war, however, for some sort of education. The Ordinance of 1785 reserved land for schools in every township, and the Northwest Ordinance of 1787 mandated schools as part of new territories and states.

10. Butts, *The American Tradition*, 15, 19, 22–23, 26; Fraser, *Between Church and State*, 10; Robert S. Michaelsen, *Piety in the Public School: Trends and Issues in the Relationship Between Religion and the Public School in the United States* (New York: Macmillan, 1970), 49.

11. Butts, *The American Tradition*, 66–67.

12. Warren A. Nord, *Religion and American Education: Rethinking a National Dilemma* (Chapel Hill: University of North Carolina Press, 1995), 63, 64; Sherry L. Field, "Historical Perspective on Character Education," *The Educational Forum* 60 (1996): 118–23; David Tyack, *Seeking Common Ground: Public Schools in a Diverse Society* (Cambridge, MA: Harvard University Press, 2003).

13. Carl F. Kaestle, *Pillars of the Republic: Common Schools and American Society, 1780–1860* (New York: Hill and Wang, 1983), 79; Stephen Macedo, *Diversity and Distrust: Civic Education in a Multicultural Democracy* (Cambridge, MA: Harvard University Press, 2000), 48–49; Jeff Archer, "Uncommon Values," *Education Week* 19, no. 8 (October 20, 1999): 26–32; Charles L. Glenn Jr., *The Myth of the Common School* (Amherst: University of Massachusetts Press, 1988), 158.

14. McClellan, *Moral Education in America*, 33; Catharine Beecher, *A Treatise on Domestic Economy* (New York: Marsh, Capen, Lyon, and Webb, 1841), 2; The greater disparity between students' values and cultures and that of pan-Protestantism, the more oppressive this education became. Perhaps the most extreme example was the particularly brutal and immoral "education" of American Indians. K. Tsianina Lomawaima describes the process: "Tribal/communal identity, primitive language, heathen religion: these pernicious influences would be rooted out and effaced in the construction of a new kind of American citizen" (K. Tsianina Lomawaima, *They Called It Prairie Light: The Story of Chilocco Indian School* (Lincoln: University of Nebraska Press, 1994), xi).

15. Glenn, *The Myth of the Common School*, 188; William J. Reese, "Public Schools and the Elusive Search for the Common Good," in *Reconstructing the Common Good in Education: Coping with Intractable American Dilemmas*, ed. Larry Cuban and Dorothy Shipps, 20 (Stanford, CA: Stanford University Press, 2000); David B. Tyack and Elisabeth Hansot, *Managers of Virtue: Public School Leadership in America, 1820–1980* (New York: Basic Books, 1982; McClellan, *Moral Education in America*, 35; Jeffrey J. Pyle, "Socrates, the Schools, and Civility: The Continuing War between Inculcation and Inquiry," *Journal of Law and Education* 26, no. 1 (1997): 69.

16. Michaelsen, *Piety in the Public School*, 84; Fraser, *Between Church and State*, 67, 77–81.

17. Kaestle, *Pillars of the Republic*, 116; Glenn, *The Myth of the Common School*, 10, 219–20.

18. Tyack and Hansot, *Managers of Virtue*, 3; Kaestle, *Pillars of the Republic*, 122.

19. David Tyack, "The Kingdom of God and the Common School," *The Harvard Educational Review* 36, no. 4 (1966): 450–55, 466.

20. Macedo, *Diversity and Distrust*, 57.

21. Tyack and Hansot, *Managers of Virtue*, 21–22; Kaestle, *Pillars of the Republic*, 168–70.

22. David Tyack, Thomas James, and Aaron Benavot, *Law and the Shaping of Public Education, 1785–1954* (Madison: University of Wisconsin Press, 1987), 162; McClellan, *Moral Education in America*, 37; Fraser, *Between Church and State*, 49.

23. Tyack, "Onward Christian Soldiers," 221, 223; National Teachers' Association, *Proceedings* (New York: C. W. Bardeen, 1869), 725; E. E. White, "Religion in the School," *Proceedings of the International Congress of Education* (New York: National Education Association, 1894), 299–300.

24. Benjamin James Justice, "Peaceable Adjustments: Religious Diversity and Local Control in New York State Public Schools, 1865–1900" (Ph.D. diss., Stanford University, 2002); Benjamin Justice, *The War that Wasn't: Religious Conflict and Compromise in the Common Schools of New York State, 1865–1900* (Albany: State University of New York Press, 2005); Tyack et al., *Law and the Shaping of Public Education*, 162, 163; Tyack, "Onward Christian Soldiers," 225; R. Laurence Moore argues that Bible reading was uncommon in nineteenth-century public schools nationwide, but his claims also rely on self-reporting from teachers and districts who may have underemphasized such curricular elements to avoid controversy ("Bible Reading and Nonsectarian Schooling: The Failure of Religious Instruction in Nineteenth-Century Public Education," *The Journal of American History* 86, no. 4 (2000): 1581–99).

25. Michaelsen, *Piety in the Public School*, 168; *Donahoe v. Richards*, 38 Me. 379 (1854); Tyack et al., *Law and the Shaping of Public Education*, 163; Joan DelFattore, *The Fourth R: Conflicts over Religion in America's Public Schools* (New Haven, CT: Yale University Press, 2004), 44.

26. *Board of Education of the City of Cincinnati v. Minor et al.*, 23 Ohio St. 211 (1872), 250–51; Regarding the exclusionary nature of pan-Protestant assumptions, Judge Welch observed:

> If, by this generic word "religion," was really meant "the Christian religion," or "Bible religion," why was it not plainly so written? Surely the subject was of importance enough to justify the pains. . . . Neither the word "Christianity," "Christian," nor "Bible" is to be found in either [our state or federal Constitution]. When they speak of "religion," they must mean the religion of man, and not the religion of any class of men. When they speak of "all men" having certain

rights, they cannot mean merely "all Christian men." Some of the very men who helped to frame these constitutions were themselves not Christian men. (246)

See also Butts, *The American Tradition*, 142; Michaelsen, *Piety in the Public School*, 89–98.

27. Samuel Windsor Brown, *The Secularization of American Education: As Shown By State Legislation, State Constitutional Provisions and State Supreme Court Decisions* (New York: Teachers College, 1912); Nord, *Religion and American Education*, 96; DelFattore, *The Fourth R*, 55–61; for the secularization argument, see also Fraser, *Between Church and State*, 114–15; Michaelsen, *Piety in the Public School*, 109–12; *Weiss v. the District Board of Edgerton*, 76 Wis. 177 (1890), 194.

28. James S. Leming, "In Search of Effective Character Education," *Educational Leadership* 51 (1993): 69; McClellan, *Moral Education in America*, 49–50; Glenn, *The Myth of the Common School*, 188; the NEA's common core approach was ultimately rejected by the American Council on Education in 1947.

29. Wilford Merton Aikin, *The Story of the Eight-Year Study, with Conclusions and Recommendations* (New York: Harper and Brothers, 1942), 1, 2, 138; McClellan, *Moral Education in America*, 60; Bruce R. Thomas, "The School As a Moral Learning Community," in *The Moral Dimensions of Teaching*, ed. John I. Goodlad, Roger Soder, and Kenneth A. Sirotnik, 278 (San Francisco: Jossey-Bass, 1990).

30. William Sherman Fleming, *God in Our Public Schools* (Pittsburgh, PA: The National Reform Association, 1947), 80, 158, emphasis in original.

31. McClellan, *Moral Education in America*, 62; Michaelsen, *Piety in the Public School*, 168; Tyack, "Onward Christian Soldiers," 243.

32. Fraser, *Between Church and State*, 118, 121–26; Garry Wills, *Under God: Religion and American Politics* (New York: Simon and Schuster, 1990), 113.

33. *Illinois ex rel. McCollum v. Board of Education*, 333 U.S. 203 (1948), 465–66; The Supreme Court decision four years later in *Zorach v. Clauson*, 343 U.S. 306 (1952)—affirming that students could be excused for religious instruction off campus—made the continuation of released time less of a legal risk, and the practice actually continued to grow in the 1950s (Zimmerman, *Whose America?*, 152).

34. Ronald F. Thiemann, "Public Religion: Bane or Blessing for Democracy?," in *Obligations of Citizenship and Demands of Faith: Religious Accommodation in Pluralist Democracies*, ed. Nancy L. Rosenblum, 80 (Princeton, NJ: Princeton University Press, 2000).

35. Zimmerman, *Whose America?*, 138, 163; DelFattore, *The Fourth R*, 68–69; Tyack, "Onward Christian Soldiers," 243; Another related tension between national unity and individual rights played out a decade earlier in two Supreme Court flag salute decisions. In *Minersville v. Gobitis*, 310 US 586 (1940), two Jehovah's Witness siblings refused to salute the flag for religious reasons, and the Court agreed that the priority of civic socialization trumped their freedom of religion. In a similar case just three years later—in *West Virginia State Board of Education v. Barnette*, 319 US 624 (1943)—the Court admitted frankly that the *Gobitis* case had been "wrongly decided," and that the state has no business prescribing confessions of orthodoxy.

36. *Engel v. Vitale*, 370 U.S. 421 (1962), 604–605; Fraser, *Between Church and State*, 146–48; *School District of Abington Township, Pennsylvania v. Schempp*, 374 US 203 (1963); a footnote in *Engel*, however, did leave open the idea that patriotic rituals referring to God or religion would be acceptable; this allowance for religious references in patriotic, school-sponsored exercises remains a central claim in the ongoing defense of "under God" in the Pledge of Allegiance.

37. Zimmerman, *Whose America?*, 164–67, 174–75; Fraser, *Between Church and State*, 150, 175; Beginning in 1961, three Supreme Court cases in the space of a decade addressed the question of what counts as a religion. I address this issue in more detail in chapter 3, but it is worth noting in the context of this historical analysis that these decisions resulted in a broadened legal view of religion, including nontheistic beliefs and sincerely held equivalents to religious belief.

38. Michaelsen, *Piety in the Public School*, 219 (pamphlet issued by the United Presbyterian Church in the United States of America, Office of the General Assembly, Philadelphia, PA, 7, 12); Liberals had other reasons to keep quiet about the judicial rulings, however. Many liberals who supported ecumenical religious instruction or observance in public schools now felt impelled to abandon this cause, for fear of calling into question the Supreme Court's authority on racial matters such as the *Brown* decision; segregationists, in contrast, seized upon the general anger over *Schempp* to decry the Court's influence across the board, and particularly in *Brown* (see Zimmerman, *Whose America?*, 161; DelFattore, *The Fourth R*, 61–64).

39. *School District of Abington Township, Pennsylvania v. Schempp*, 374 US 203 (1963), 225; Michaelsen, *Piety in the Public School*, 213; Nord, *Religion and American Education*, 115.

40. Louis Edward Raths, Merrill Harmin, and Sidney B. Simon, *Values and Teaching: Working with Values in the Classroom* (Columbus, OH: C. E. Merrill Books, 1966); B. Edward McClellan observes that the 1960s—with the rise of relativism and the antiauthoritarian stance of many educational reformers—provided fertile ground for the emergence of values clarification: "Americans lost faith in the ability to find common ground" and sought to maintain a "fragile peace by accepting differences and encouraging tolerance" (*Moral Education in America*, 75–76).

41. James S. Leming, "Research and Practice in Character Education: A Historical Perspective," in *The Construction of Children's Character: Ninety-Sixth Yearbook of the National Society for the Study of Education*, part II, ed. Alex Molnar, 31–44 (Chicago: University of Chicago Press, 1997); for examples of specific critiques, see Dwight Boyd and Deanne Bogdan, "'Something' Clarified, Nothing of 'Value': A Rhetorical Critique of Values Clarification," *Educational Theory* 34, no. 3 (1984): 287–300, and Alan L. Lockwood, "A Critical View of Values Clarification," *Teachers College Record* 77, no. 1 (1975): 35–50.

42. Thomas Lickona, *Educating for Character: How Our Schools Can Teach Respect and Responsibility* (New York: Bantam Books, 1991), 11.

43. Marvin Berkowitz, "The Science of Character Education," in *Bringing in a New Era*, 56; For critiques of Kohlberg's model of abstract justice and, in particular, the use of moral dilemmas, see Audrey Thompson, "The Baby with a Gun: A Feminist Inquiry into

Plausibility, Certainty, and Context in Moral Education," in *Philosophy of Education 1990*, ed. David P. Ericson, 241–42 (Urbana, IL: Philosophy of Education Society, 1991); Carol Gilligan, *In a Different Voice: Psychological Theory and Women's Development* (Cambridge, MA: Harvard University Press, 1982); Nel Noddings, *Caring: A Feminine Approach to Ethics and Moral Education* (Berkeley: University of California Press, 1984).

44. Richard A. Shweder, Manamohan Mahapatra, and Joan G. Miller, "Culture and Moral Development," in *Cultural Psychology: Essays on Comparative Human Development*, ed. James W. Stigler, Richard A. Shweder, and Gilbert H. Herdt, 130–204 (Cambridge: Cambridge University Press, 1990); William Damon, "Character Study," *Responsive Community* 11, no. 2 (2001): 64–65; Daniel Pekarsky, "Moral Choice and Education," *Journal of Moral Education* 12, no. 1 (1983): 8; James R. Rest, "Notes for an Aspiring Researcher in Moral Development Theory & Practice," *Moral Education Forum* 20, no. 4 (1995): 11–14; James R. Rest et al., "A Neo-Kohlbergian Approach to Morality Research," *Journal of Moral Education* 29, no. 4 (2000): 381–95; Donald R. C. Reed, *Following Kohlberg: Liberalism and the Practice of Democratic Community* (Notre Dame, IN: University of Notre Dame Press, 1997), xiii; Leming, "Research and Practice," 31–44; John Snarey and Thomas Pavkov, "Moral Character Education in the United States: Beyond Socialization versus Development," in *Learning for Life: Moral Education Theory and Practice*, ed. Andrew Garrod, 25–46 (Westport, CT: Praeger, 1992); McClellan, *Moral Education in America*, 83; McClellan notes that Kohlberg later acknowledges that his earlier model was "not a sufficient guide to the moral educator who deals with the moral concrete in a school world in which value content as well as structure, behavior as well as reasoning, must be dealt with" (Lawrence Kohlberg, "Moral Education Reappraised," *The Humanist* 38 (November 1978): 14.

45. As of October 2001, at least forty states were actively involved in character education efforts through legislative mandates or federal grants (see Haynes and Thomas, *Finding Common Ground*, 159; Character Education Partnership, http://www.character.org); Thomas Lickona, "Religion and Character Education," *Phi Delta Kappan* 81, no. 1 (1999): 23. Some character education curricula do have relatively direct ties with religion, such as Character First!, a division of a Christian ministry organization based in Illinois.

46. Warren Nord, "Moral Disagreement, Moral Education, Common Ground," in *Making Good Citizens: Education and Civil Society*, ed. Diane Ravitch and Joseph P. Viteritti, 146 (New Haven, CT: Yale University Press, 2001); David E. Purpel, "The Politics of Character Education," *The Construction of Children's Character*, part II, ed. Alex Molnar, 150 (Chicago: University of Chicago Press, 1997); Willem L. Wardekker, "Schools and Moral Education: Conformism or Autonomy?," *Journal of Philosophy of Education* 35, no. 1 (2001): 105.

47. Muriel J. Bebeau, James R. Rest, and Darcia Narvaez, "Beyond the Promise: A Perspective on Research in Moral Education," *Educational Researcher* 28, no. 4 (1999): 20; see also Susan Black, "The Character Conundrum," *The American School Board Journal* 10, no. 1 (1996): 29–31; David Brooks and Mark E. Kann, "What Makes Character Education Programs Work?" *Educational Leadership* 51 (1993): 21; Simon, *Moral Questions in the Classroom*, 172–87.

48. *Lemon v. Kurtzman*, 403 US 602 (1971), 612–13.

49. *Tinker v. Des Moines Independent Community School Dist.*, 393 U.S. 503 (1968), 508–509; DelFattore, *The Fourth R*, 258–59; Kent Greenawalt, *Does God Belong in Public Schools?* (Princeton, NJ: Princeton University Press, 2005), 20; Jeffrey Rosen, "Is Nothing Secular?" *New York Times Magazine* (January 30, 2000): 40–45.

50. Ironically, the strategy of "equal time" emerged in part from a Supreme Court rejection of a state prohibition against teaching evolution; Justice Fortas's majority opinion created an unintentional loophole by claiming that the government's programs or practices cannot "aid or oppose" religion: "This prohibition is absolute. It forbids alike the preference of a religious doctrine or the prohibition of theory which is deemed antagonistic to a particular dogma." This loophole has been used by conservative Christian groups arguing that "creation science" should be included in the curriculum (see Fraser, *Between Church and State*, 158–61; *Epperson v. Arkansas*, 393 US 97 (1968), 106–07; Zimmerman, *Whose America?*, 6).

51. Michaelsen, *Piety in the Public School*, 200.

CHAPTER 3

1. Stephen L. Darwall, "Two Kinds of Respect," in *Dignity, Character, and Self-Respect*, ed. Robin S. Dillon, 183, 192 (New York: Routledge, 1995).

2. Loren E. Lomasky, *Persons, Rights, and the Moral Community* (New York: Oxford University Press, 1987), 26; Lomasky includes a detailed argument for why children and mentally/physically disabled individuals share the status of project pursuers, even while many of them do not pursue projects themselves.

3. Gregory Vlastos, "Justice and Equality," in *Social Justice*, ed. Richard B. Brandt and Kenneth Ewart Boulding, 44 (Englewood Cliffs, NJ: Prentice Hall, 1962).

4. Mark H. Davis et al., "Effect of Perspective Taking on the Cognitive Representation of Persons: A Merging of Self and Others," *Journal of Personality and Social Psychology* 70, no. 4 (1996): 713.

5. William A. Galston, *Liberal Pluralism: The Implications of Value Pluralism for Political Theory and Practice* (Cambridge: Cambridge University Press, 2002), 119–20; John Rawls, *Political Liberalism* (New York: Columbia University Press, 1993), 158ff.

6. Charles Taylor, *Sources of the Self: The Making of the Modern Identity* (Cambridge, MA: Harvard University Press, 1989), 27; Charles Taylor, "Two Theories of Modernity," *The Responsive Community* 6, no. 3 (1996): 47.

7. For a more developed argument along these lines, see Thomas E. Hill Jr., *Respect for Humanity*, ed. Grethe B. Petersen, vol. 18 of *The Tanner Lectures on Human Values* (Salt Lake City: University of Utah Press, 1997), 25.

8. Hill, *Respect for Humanity*, 32–33.

9. Eamonn Callan, "Tradition and Integrity in Moral Education," *American Journal of Education* 101 (1992): 4.

10. See, for example, the University of Illinois at Chicago's Office of Studies in Moral Development and Education (http://tigger.uic.edu/~lnucci/MoralEd/), particularly research and curricula related to domain theory.

11. *United States v. Seeger*, 380 US 163 (1968), 165–66; *Welsh v. United States*, 398 US 333 (1970), 333–34.

12. Paul Tillich, *Christianity and the Encounter of the World Religions* (New York: Columbia University Press, 1963), 4–6; *Mozert v. Hawkins County Board of Education*, 827 F.2d 1058 (1987); David Ruenzel, "The Spirit of Waldorf Education," *Education Week* 20, no. 41 (June 20, 2001): 38–45.

13. Not all religions include a comprehensive ethical framework; Buddhist traditions are arguably the most prominent examples of this (although some modern Buddhist scholars and adherents have sought to extrapolate ethical principles). This should serve to remind us of the great diversity within the religious domain as well, and the inadvisability of seeking an essentialist definition.

14. Richard N. Ostling, "America's Ever-Changing Religious Landscape," *Brookings Review* 17, no. 2 (1999): 11, 13; for survey examples, see "The American Religious Landscape and Politics," a poll conducted by the Pew Forum on Religion and Public Life, March–May 2004, and "Exploring Religious America," a poll conducted for *Religion & Ethics Newsweekly* and *U.S. News & World Report* (March 26–April 4, 2002), by Mitofsky International and Edison Media Research; Thiemann, "Public Religion," 78–79.

15. Diana L. Eck, *A New Religious America: How a "Christian Country" Has Now Become the World's Most Religious Diverse Nation* (New York: HarperSanFrancisco, 2001), 46, 4; Warren A. Nord and Charles C. Haynes affirm Eck's contention (*Taking Religion Seriously across the Curriculum* (Alexandria, VA: Association of Supervision and Curriculum Development, 1998), 68).

16. Immigration is changing the face of religious America, Jenkins asserts, but it is the influence of Latino immigration on the Christian church—especially its evangelical and Catholic forms—that will likely bring greater change. Unlike in the past, Jenkins notes, new ethnic immigrants are not simply assimilating into mainstream churches (Philip Jenkins, "Here For Good: Religion and the New Immigrants," *Books and Culture* 8, no. 3 [2002]: 12–13); Roberto S. Goizueta, *Caminemos con Jesús: Toward a Hispanic/Latino Theology of Accompaniment* (Maryknoll, NY: Orbis, 1995); Eck, *A New Religious America*, 383; Allen Figueroa Deck, "The Challenge of Evangelical/Pentecostal Christianity to Hispanic Catholicism," in *Religion in American Culture*, ed. David G. Hackett, 461–77 (New York: Routledge, 1995).

17. Here we should also keep in mind that religious diversity varies widely by region. In some places—such as Eck's cosmopolitan Cambridge surroundings—a rich variety of religions and religious skepticism abounds. In others, Christianity remains the overwhelmingly dominant framework. Even in these latter regions, however, students are citizens of a broader national polity and thus still share the burden of understanding significant ethical diversity.

18. "America's Struggle with Religion's Role at Home and Abroad," a poll conducted by the Pew Research Center for the People and the Press and Pew Forum on Religion and Public Life, February 25–March 10, 2002.

19. Often based on attendance at religious services, these figures may very well underestimate religions that do not operate with a model of regular congregational gathering. Furthermore, general surveys provide accurate estimates of large subpopulations (such as European-origin Catholics and Baptists), but not so with small ones (such as Jews and Muslims) or populations not fluent in English (see R. Stephen Warner and Judith G. Wittner, *Gatherings in Diaspora: Religious Communities and the New Immigration* (Philadelphia: Temple University Press, 1998), 11).

20. Robert Wuthnow, *After Heaven: Spirituality in America Since the 1950s* (Berkeley, CA: University of California Press, 1993), 3; for examples, see Richard Higgins, "Sold on Spirituality," *Boston Globe Magazine* (December 3, 2000, 19–24); also see Mark Mittelburg and Bill Hybels, *Building Contagious Churches* (Grand Rapids, MI: Zondervan, 2000). Interestingly, some recent research suggests that this seeker mentality is less prevalent among adolescents, who appear to be "mostly oriented toward and engaged in conventional religious tradition and communities" (Christian Smith, *Soul Searching: The Religious Lives of American Teenagers* (New York: Oxford University Press, 2005), 27). It may be, however, that spiritual seeking increases later (as Smith himself acknowledges), especially for those attending college.

21. Glenn, *The Myth of the Common School*, xi; Mary Ann Zehr, "Evangelical Christian Schools See Growth," *Education Week* 24, no. 15 (December 8, 2004): 1, 17; National Center for Education Statistics, *1.1 Million Homeschooled Students in the United States in 2003* (Washington, DC: NCES Publication No. 2004115, 2004).

22. Warner and Wittner, *Gatherings in Diaspora*; Helen Rose Fuchs Ebaugh and Janet Saltzman Chafetz, *Religion and the New Immigrants: Continuities and Adaptations in Immigrant Congregations* (Walnut Creek, CA: AltaMira Press, 2000), 18.

23. Goizueta, *Caminemos con Jesús*, 50, 56.

24. Rupert Gethin, *The Foundations of Buddhism* (Oxford: Oxford University Press, 1998), 138–39; see also David Tracy, *Dialogue with the Other: The Inter-Religious Dialogue* (Grand Rapids, MI: Eerdmans, 1990), 47.

25. This rationale may prove uncompelling to a Buddhist, but it seems likely that many such frameworks will find other motivations to engage in Ethical Dialogue. For some Buddhists, at least, the notion of universal oneness might provide reason to treat all lives with respect and a desire to understand them in their various forms. For Christians and Jews, the belief that we are all created in God's image and thus carry unique value may serve as a compelling justification for mutual respect (for Muslims, the sentiment would be similar, although with less anthropomorphic imagery).

26. Willem L. Wardekker and Siebren Miedema, "Denominational School Identity and the Formation of Personal Identity," *Religious Education* 96, no. 1 (2001): 37.

27. For a theoretical argument along these lines, see Larry P. Nucci, *Education in the Moral Domain* (Cambridge: Cambridge University Press, 2001), chapter 2; for an extended critique of Nucci's argument, see my article, "Religion, Ethics, and the Implications for Moral Education: A Critique of Nucci's 'Morality and Religious Rules,'" *Journal of Moral Education* 32, no. 3 (2003): 251–61.

28. Eamonn Callan, "Godless Moral Education and Liberal Tolerance," *Journal of Philosophy of Education* 23, no. 2 (1989): 273.

29. Benjamin R. Barber, "America Skips School," *Harper's Magazine* (November 1993): 43.

CHAPTER 4

1. I use the term *civic* to denote the realm of our life together outside of private (familial, religious, etc.) associations. I will develop this distinction further in chapter 5, when I focus on deliberation in the civic realm.

2. Nord, *Religion and American Education*, 214.

3. Deborah Kerdeman, "Between Interlochen and Idaho: Hermeneutics and Education for Understanding," in *Philosophy of Education 1998*, ed. Steven Tozer, 275 (Urbana, IL: Philosophy of Education Society, 1999).

4. Clifford Geertz, *Local Knowledge: Further Essays in Interpretive Anthropology* (New York: Basic Books, 1983), 44; While his focus is on the somewhat narrower concept of historical empathy, Stuart Foster offers substantive evidence that students are able to improve their understanding of human actions in the past (see Stuart J. Foster, "Historical Empathy in Theory and Practice: Some Final Thoughts," in *Historical Empathy and Perspective Taking in the Social Studies*, ed. O. L. Davis, Elizabeth Anne Yeager, and Stuart J. Foster, 180, footnote 22 (Lanham, MD: Rowman and Littlefield, 2001).

5. Martin L. Hoffman, *Empathy and Moral Development: Implications for Caring and Social Justice* (Cambridge: Cambridge University Press, 2000); Berkowitz, "The Science of Character Education," 52; For a thoughtful critique of Piaget's and Kohlberg's constructs involving egocentric thinking in young children, see Michael S. Pritchard, *Reasonable Children: Moral Education and Moral Learning* (Lawrence, KS: University Press of Kansas, 1996), chapter 8.

6. Goizueta, *Caminemos con Jesús*, 154.

7. Uma Narayan, "Working Together across Difference: Some Considerations on Emotions and Political Practice," *Hypatia* 3, no. 2 (1988): 31–47.

8. Elliot Turiel, "Conflict, Social Development, and Cultural Change," in *Development and Cultural Change: Reciprocal Processes*, ed. Elliot Turiel, 77–92 (San Francisco: Jossey-Bass, 1999); Walter C. Parker, "The Deliberative Approach to Democratic Education: Problems and Possibilities," *School Field* 13, no. 3–4: 25–42.

9. John Stuart Mill, *Utilitarianism: On Liberty; Considerations on Representative Government; Remarks on Bentham's Philosophy*, ed. Geraint Williams, 116 (London: Dent, 1993); bell hooks, *Teaching to Transgress: Education As the Practice of Freedom* (New York: Routledge, 1994), 88; hooks quotes Giroux from "The Hope of Radical Education: A Conversation with Henry Giroux," *Journal of Education* 170, no. 2 (1988): 91–101.

10. Vivian Gussin Paley, *Kwanzaa and Me: A Teacher's Story* (Cambridge, MA: Harvard University Press, 1995), 56, 117, emphasis in original; Kenneth A. Strike, "Ethical

Discourse and Pluralism," in *Ethics for Professionals in Education: Perspectives for Preparation and Practice*, ed. Kenneth A. Strike and P. Lance Ternasky, 186 (New York: Teachers College Press, 1993).

11. For a thoughtful analysis of this issue, see Nicole Bishop, "Trust Is Not Enough: Classroom Self-Disclosure and the Loss of Private Lives," *Journal of Philosophy of Education* 30, no. 3 (1996): 435.

12. Robert J. Nash, *Religious Pluralism in the Academy: Opening the Dialogue* (New York: P. Lang, 2001), 45. Even when students are not directly involved in the expression of their private ethical frameworks, exploring them deserves special care, as Kenneth Strike points out: "Especially when we are dealing with young minds, we need to proceed with a higher level of sensitivity than may be required by treating the issues as solely issues of intellectual liberty. We are discussing matters that are of more moment to people than, say, different interpretations of theories of gravitation" (Kenneth A. Strike, "Are Secular Ethical Languages Religiously Neutral?," *Journal of Law and Politics* 6 (1999): 489).

13. Ellen Sorokin, "California School Sued over Islamic Drills," *Washington Times*, July 10, 2002, p. AO3; Interestingly, this lawsuit was dismissed in a summary judgment by the Ninth Circuit Court (an appeal remains pending). The decision apparently hinged on whether the curriculum aimed at indoctrination, but my point here is that—regardless of the intent—several activities involved enactment of religious ritual, however fragmentary. Whether the unit was ultimately illegal is perhaps contestable, but certainly there were more sensitive, and ultimately more educationally potent, ways to engage students in the subject.

14. See, for example, Richard J. Kraft and James C. Kielsmeier, eds., *Experiential Learning in Schools and Higher Education* (Boulder, CO: Association for Experiential Education, 1995); Bettina Hansel, *The AFS Impact Study: Final Report* (New York: AFS International/Intercultural Programs, 1986).

15. Maxine Greene, *Releasing the Imagination: Essays on Education, the Arts, and Social Change* (San Francisco: Jossey-Bass, 1995), 125.

16. For philosophical arguments on the value of ethical exemplars, see Jeffrey Stout, *Ethics after Babel: The Languages of Morals and Their Discontents* (Boston: Beacon Press, 1988); Lee H. Yearley, "Conflicts among Ideals of Human Flourishing," in *Prospects for a Common Morality*, ed. Gene H. Outka and John P. Reeder, 233–53 (Princeton, NJ: Princeton University Press, 1993); Walker, "Moral Exemplarity," in *Bringing in a New Era*, 81, 82; One particularly promising curricular example is from the Giraffe Heroes Program, which focuses on "people who stick their necks out for the common good" but also provides developmentally appropriate encouragement for students to see heroes not as larger than life but as everyday people who inspire others.

17. Hilary E. Davis, "If Art Is Good for the Soul, Can Education Do without Art?," in *Philosophy of Education 1997*, ed. Susan Laird, 285–88 (Urbana, IL: Philosophy of Education Society, 1998); for additional commentary on the limitations of art in fostering interpersonal understanding, see Elaine Scarry, "The Difficulty of Imagining Other People," in *For Love of Country: Debating the Limits of Patriotism*, ed. Martha Nussbaum and Joshua Cohen, 98–110 (Boston: Beacon Press, 1996); Susan Verducci, "Moral Empathy:

The Necessity of Intersubjectivity and Dialogic Confirmation," in *Philosophy of Education 1998*, ed. Steven Tozer, 335–42 (Urbana, IL.: Philosophy of Education Society, 1999); Susan Verducci, "A Conceptual History of Empathy and a Question It Raises for Moral Education," *Educational Theory* 50, no. 1 (2000): 63–80.

18. Susan L. Douglass, *Teaching about Religion in National and State Social Studies Standards* (Fountain Valley, CA: Council on Islamic Education and First Amendment Center, 2000), 93–94; See also Nord and Haynes, *Taking Religion Seriously*, 78–80; In a January 2001 poll, 69 percent of public school teachers acknowledged that they were "not at all familiar" with guidelines on religious expression in schools distributed by the Clinton administration the year prior (see Robert C. Johnston, "Schools Fall Short on First Amendment Rights," *Education Week* (March 21, 2001): 5).

19. Patricia G. Avery, "Political Tolerance: How Adolescents Deal with Dissenting Groups," in *The Development of Political Understanding*, ed. Helen Haste and Judith Torney-Purta, 41, 49 (San Francisco: Jossey-Bass, 1992); Michael Schleifer, "The Effect of Philosophical Discussions in the Classroom on Respect for Others and Non-Stereotypic Attitudes," *Thinking: The Journal of Philosophy for Children* 12, no. 4 (1996): 34; Robert DeHaan et al., "Promoting Ethical Reasoning, Affect, and Behavior among High School Students: An Evaluation of Three Teaching Strategies," *Journal of Moral Education* 26, no. 1 (1997): 5–20; see also Diana Hess, "Dilemmas of Democracy Education: The Strengths and Shortfalls of Controversial Public Issues Discussion" (paper presented at the annual meeting of the American Educational Research Association, New Orleans, LA, April 2, 2002).

20. Parker, "The Deliberative Approach," 7.

21. Strike, "Secular Ethical Languages," 501–502.

22. Simon, *Moral Questions*, 211, 237.

23. Eamonn Callan, "Common Schools for Common Education," *Canadian Journal of Education* 20, no. 3 (1995): 269–70.

CHAPTER 5

1. I use the term *liberal* throughout this book in the way political theorists do, involving a strong commitment to individual liberties; in this broad sense, it encompasses the more common usages of liberal (e.g., Democrat) and conservative (e.g., Republican).

2. While most liberal political theory uses the term *public* to denote the *political* (e.g., "public reason"), this strikes me as potentially misleading. In common parlance, the idea of our public life together includes far more than just the exercise of state power. Instead I find the distinction between the broader civic realm and the narrowly political to be crucial in emphasizing the importance of cross-group civic dialogue that doesn't involve the use of state power. This distinction is also drawn in Seyla Benhabib, *Democracy and Difference: Contesting the Boundaries of the Political* (Princeton, NJ: Princeton University Press, 1996); David Hollenbach, "Contexts of the Political Role of Religion: Civil Society and Culture," in *Reasonable Pluralism*, ed. Paul J. Weithman, 269–93 (New

York: Garland, 1999); and Kenneth A. Strike, "On the Construction of Public Speech," *Educational Theory* 44, no. 1 (1994): 1–25.

3. See, for example, Stephen Holmes, *Passions and Constraint* (Chicago: University of Chicago Press, 1995), chapter 7; most of these arguments extend the restriction to any "private languages," of which religious is the most prominent example.

4. Stephen Macedo, "Liberal Civic Education and Religious Fundamentalism: The Case of God v. John Rawls?" *Ethics* 105 (1995): 479–80.

5. Nicholas Wolterstorff, *Religion in the Public Square: The Place of Religious Convictions in Political Debate*, ed. Robert Audi and Nicholas Wolterstorff, 111 (Lanham, MD: Rowman and Littlefield, 1997).

6. Throughout this chapter, I am making a normative argument about what is required for civic virtue, not advocating that the requirements of reasonableness, respect, and so on should be legal thresholds to political participation.

7. Rawls, *Political Liberalism*, 15–18, 49–50. Reciprocity is, by definition, a bilateral endeavor; to abide by rules of cooperation while being exploited would neglect an equally important respect for oneself.

8. Rawls, *Political Liberalism*, 54–58.

9. See Amy Gutmann and Dennis Thompson, "Deliberative Democracy beyond Process," *The Journal of Political Philosophy* 10, no. 2 (2002): 153–74.

10. Stephen Macedo, "Liberal Civic Education and Its Limits," *Canadian Journal of Education* 20, no. 3 (1995): 313.

11. Hoffman, *Empathy and Moral Development*, 63–92; John Deigh, "Empathy and Universalizability," *Ethics* 105, no. 4 (1995): 760; Robert L. Selman, "Social-Cognitive Understanding," in *Moral Development and Behavior: Theory, Research, and Social Issues*, ed. Thomas Lickona, 304 (New York: Holt, Rinehart, and Winston, 1976).

12. Charles Larmore, "Pluralism and Reasonable Disagreement," *Social Philosophy and Policy* 11, no. 1 (1994): 66.

13. Jeffrey Stout, *Democracy and Tradition* (Princeton, NJ: Princeton University Press, 2004), 298.

14. Will Kymlicka, "Education for Citizenship," in *Education in Morality*, ed. J. Mark Halstead and Terence H. McLaughlin, 89 (London: Routledge, 1999).

15. Natasha Levinson, "Deliberative Democracy and Justice," in *Philosophy of Education 2001*, ed. Suzanne Rice, 57 (Urbana, IL: Philosophy of Education Society, 2002).

16. Iris Marion Young, "Activist Challenges to Deliberative Democracy," *Political Theory* 29, no. 5 (2001): 686; Lisa D. Delpit, "The Silenced Dialogue: Power and Pedagogy in Educating Other People's Children," *Harvard Educational Review* 58, no. 3 (1988): 280–98.

17. Paley, *Kwanzaa and Me*, 9; Vivian Gussin Paley, *You Can't Say You Can't Play* (Cambridge, MA: Harvard University Press, 1992), 56.

18. Nel Noddings, "Conversation As Moral Education," *Journal of Moral Education* 23, no. 2 (1994): 107–18; Nel Noddings, *The Challenge to Care in Schools: An Alternative Approach to Education* (New York: Teachers College Press, 1992); Callan, *Creating Citizens: Political Education and Liberal Democracy* (New York: Oxford University Press, 1997), 204.

19. Deborah Tannen, "Agonism in the Academy: Surviving Higher Learning's Argument Culture," *The Chronicle of Higher Education* 46, no. 30 (2000): B7–B8.

20. Young, "Activist Challenges," 689; Benjamin DeMott, "Seduced By Civility: Political Manners and the Crisis of Democratic Values," *The Nation* (December 9, 1996): 11–19.

21. Nash, *Religious Pluralism*, 45; Cheshire Calhoun, "The Virtue of Civility," *Philosophy and Public Affairs* 29, no. 3 (2000): 275.

22. Parker J. Palmer, *To Know As We Are Known: A Spirituality of Education* (San Francisco: Harper and Row, 1983), 74.

23. Hess, "Dilemmas of Democracy Education," 10.

24. Noddings, "Conversation As Moral Education," 110.

25. Deborah Tannen, *The Argument Culture: Moving from Debate to Dialogue* (New York: Random House, 1998), 257, 285.

26. See, for example, Walter C. Parker, "The Art of Deliberation," *Educational Leadership* 54, no. 5 (1997): 18–21; Thomas E. Kelly, "Leading Class Discussions of Controversial Issues," *Social Education* 53, no. 6 (1989): 368–70; Kenneth A. Strike, "Dialogue, Religion, and Tolerance: How to Talk to People Who Are Wrong about (Almost) Everything," in *Curriculum, Religion, and Public Education: Conversations for an Enlarging Public Square*, ed. James T. Sears and James C. Carper, 59–69 (New York: Teachers College Press, 1998); Lynn Brice, "Deliberative Discourse Enacted: Task, Text, and Talk," *Theory and Research in Social Education* 30, no. 1 (2002): 66–87; Alan Singer and Michael Pezone, "A Response to Annette Hemming's 'High School Democratic Dialogues: Possibilities for Praxis' in *American Educational Research Journal*, Spring 2000," *American Educational Research Journal* 38, no. 3 (2001): 536.

27. Kelly, "Leading Class Discussions," 368.

28. Singer and Pezone, "A Response," 537.

29. As noted earlier, the classroom episodes I share throughout this book are edited for illustrative purposes. While based on my own teaching experiences or classroom observations, most of these episodes had more fits and starts, dead ends and retries, than my brief snapshots can coherently convey. In addition, I certainly acknowledge that my attempts to foster Ethical Dialogue do not always generate this type of progress with students. At the same time, I want to reiterate that these types of conversations occur with a range of students, not simply those in "honors" or "advanced" classes.

30. Walter C. Parker, *Teaching Democracy: Unity and Diversity in Public Life* (New York: Teachers College, 2003), 3.

Chapter 6

1. "Religion and Public Life," a poll conducted by Public Agenda (New York, NY), 2000–2004, released January 23, 2005.

2. "S.C. H.S. Removes 2 Topics from Debate," Associated Press, September 30, 2004.

3. Paul J. Weithman, *Religion and the Obligations of Citizenship* (Cambridge: Cambridge University Press, 2002), 13–17, 40–48.

4. Weithman, *Religion and the Obligations of Citizenship*, 48.

5. Weithman acknowledges the value of this broader awareness as well, describing the relationship between religion and politics as *mutually* edifying. Not only can religiously-informed politics generate participation and provide new insight, he contends, but the heterogeneous milieu of political advocacy can impel religious groups to refine their positions and arguments in response to opposing viewpoints. What seems vital to me, however, is that this mutual edification be encouraged as a matter of civic virtue, not simply political expediency wherein positions are modified for tactical purposes; for a more extended analysis of Weithman's argument, see my article, "Religion, Politics, and Civic Education," *Journal of Philosophy of Education* 39, no. 1 (2005): 159–68.

6. For a compelling analysis of how Rawlsian political liberalism cannot avoid sliding into a more comprehensive framework, see Callan, *Creating Citizens*, chapter 2, and Eamonn Callan, "Liberal Legitimacy, Justice, and Civic Education," *Ethics* 111 (2000): 141–55; Veit Bader, "Religious Pluralism: Secularism or Priority for Democracy?," *Political Theory* 27, no. 5 (1999): 616; Amy Gutmann, "Challenges of Multiculturalism in Democratic Education, in *Public Education in a Multicultural Society: Policy, Theory, Critique*, ed. Robert K. Fullinwider, 168 (New York: Cambridge University Press, 1996).

7. Mark Holmes, for instance, asserts this unwarranted equivalence when he claims that "to set up 'reasonableness' as the central criterion [for political decision making] is to insist on the superiority of a non-religious creed" (see "Common Schools for a Secularist Society," *Canadian Journal of Education* 20, no. 3 (1995): 285); see also Robert Audi's argument in *Religion in the Public Square: The Place of Religious Convictions in Political Debate*, ed. Robert Audi and Nicholas Wolterstorff, 1–66 (Lanham, MD: Rowman and Littlefield, 1997); Richard A. Baer Jr., "The Supreme Court's Discriminatory Use of the Term 'Sectarian,'" *Journal of Law and Politics* 6 (1990): 461.

8. Callan, *Creating Citizens*, 37; Eamonn Callan, "Political Liberalism and Political Education," *The Review of Politics* 58, no. 1 (1996): 12.

9. Eamonn Callan, "Faith, Worship, and Reason in Religious Upbringing," *Journal of Philosophy of Education* 22, no. 2 (1988): 188, 190; Trevor Cooling, *A Christian Vision for State Education: Reflections on the Theology of Education* (London: Society for Promoting Christian Knowledge, 1994), 83.

10. Ronald F. Thiemann, "Public Religion: Bane or Blessing for Democracy?," in *Obligations of Citizenship and Demands of Faith: Religious Accommodation in Pluralist Democracies*, ed. Nancy L. Rosenblum, 87 (Princeton, NJ: Princeton University Press, 2000).

11. Charles Larmore, "Pluralism and Reasonable Disagreement," *Social Philosophy and Policy* 11, no. 1 (1994): 77. From a specifically religious standpoint, philosopher Robert Adams concurs: "There ought to be room in our conception of faith for honest investigation of all questions, and for feeling the force of objections to our faith, even while we are sustained in that faith" (*The Virtue of Faith and Other Essays in Philosophical Theology* (New York: Oxford University Press, 1987), 17).

12. For support of risk-all dialogue, see Tracy, *Dialogue with the Other*, 73; Besides the distinction between reasonableness and truth, teachers should recognize that the standards for political justification do not—and cannot, from an epistemological standpoint—apply to metaphysical beliefs. We can help students consider what convictions should be questioned and when. But there is no philosophical (and certainly no pedagogical) justification for claiming that a lack of ultimate epistemic foundation must result in total skepticism (see Mike Degenhardt, "The Ethics of Belief and the Ethics of Teaching," *Journal of Philosophy of Education* 32, no. 3 (1998): 338).

13. For a more developed critique of this "proportionality doctrine," see George I. Mavrodes, "Jerusalem and Athens Revisited," in *Faith and Rationality: Reason and Belief in God*, ed. Alvin Plantinga and Nicholas Wolterstorff, 216 (Notre Dame: University of Notre Dame Press, 1983); Adams, *The Virtue of Faith*, 18.

14. Eamonn Callan, "Autonomy, Child Rearing, and Good Lives," in *The Political and Moral Status of Children*, ed. David Archard and Colin Macleod, 127 (Oxford: Clarendon, 2001); William Galston, "Civic Education in the Liberal State," in *Philosophers on Education*, ed. Amelie Rorty, 479 (London: Routledge, 1998).

15. Nel Noddings, *Educating for Intelligent Belief or Unbelief* (New York: Teachers College Press, 1993). For an extended analysis of Noddings's approach, see my article, "Educating for More (and Less) Than Intelligent Belief or Unbelief: A Critique of Noddings's Vision of Religion in Public Schools," in *Philosophy of Education 2005* (Urbana, IL: Philosophy of Education Society, forthcoming).

16. The basic (antifoundationalist) argument here is that reason (even its scientific manifestations) is unable to confirm or deny core metaphysical beliefs such as "God exists and has this nature." At the same time, however, to acknowledge this limitation of reason is not to deny that it plays a vital role in human society and the lives of most religious adherents.

17. Callan, *Creating Citizens*, 169. This has consequences not only for schools, as Callan contends: "The severity of the contrast between the thinness of the values that are supposed to constrain my conduct *qua* citizen and the depth and richness of my ethical life, all things considered, threatens the very coherence of my moral identity" (12). It is worth pointing out that this threat is not limited to those with religious beliefs.

18. Callan, "Political Liberalism," 19.

19. Wolterstorff, *Religion in the Public Square*, 105.

20. Wolterstorff, *Religion in the Public Square*, 163.

21. Stout, *Democracy and Tradition*, 112.

22. It seems important to acknowledge that in this classroom episode, there were no Muslim students in my class. If there were, they would be a potential resource for infor-

mation and insight. But as I have observed previously, they should not be expected to serve as the definitive voice for Islam, and the degree of personal insight they provide—if any—should be at their discretion. In addition, as I acknowledged with the book's opening vignette, I have in some cases condensed these teaching episodes for simplicity of illustration. A process of Ethical Dialogue such as this one may require more time, particularly to do justice to the laying of a conceptual groundwork of different ethical frameworks and the use of various exercises and texts to spur imaginative engagement. In spite of the classroom time demands, it should be conceivable how such a process could be planned and woven into a topic of study already required for a particular curriculum. A teacher who plans examples and dilemmas for discussion in advance could certainly have her curriculum do "double duty" in exploring conceptual content while also engaging her students in Ethical Dialogue.

CHAPTER 7

1. Ana Maria Villegas and Tamara Lucas, "Preparing Culturally Responsive Teachers: Rethinking the Curriculum," *Journal of Teacher Education* 53, no. 1 (2002): 20–32; Louise B. Jennings and Cynthia Potter Smith, "Examining the Role of Critical Inquiry for Transformative Practices: Two Joint Case Studies of Multicultural Teacher Education," *Teachers College Record* 104, no. 3 (2002): 456–81.

2. Lee S. Shulman, "Knowledge and Teaching: Foundations of the New Reform," *Harvard Educational Review* 57, no. 1 (1987): 1–22.

3. David Tyack, personal conversation, April 11, 2001.

4. Noddings, *Educating for Intelligent Belief,* 123; Tracy, *Dialogue with the Other*, 55; Nord and Haynes, *Taking Religion Seriously*, 50.

5. In a 2001 poll, 69 percent of public school teachers acknowledged they were "not at all familiar" with guidelines on religious expression in schools distributed by the Clinton administration the year prior (Robert C. Johnston, "Schools Fall Short on First Amendment Rights," *Education Week* (March 21, 2001): 5; anecdotal evidence suggests a similar ignorance surrounding similar guidelines announced in February 2003 by the Bush administration.

6. Robert E. Floden, "Reforms That Call for Teaching More Than You Understand," in *Teaching and Its Predicaments*, ed. Nicholas C. Burbules and David T. Hansen, 21 (Boulder, CO: Westview Press, 1997).

7. One compelling example is the preservice program at Santa Clara University in northern California, which seeks to cultivate "informed empathy" among its teacher candidates. Through a one-week immersion experience, students are challenged to consider questions of social inequity and explore connections to classroom curricula. By encouraging an experience of imaginative engagement and continuing this focus throughout the program year, Santa Clara emphasizes a dispositional orientation toward issues that includes but extends well beyond pedagogical capacity (see Gloria Ladson-Billings, "Preparing Teachers for Diversity: Historical Perspectives, Current Trends, and Future

Directions," in *Teaching As the Learning Profession: Handbook of Policy and Practice*, ed. Linda Darling-Hammond and Gary Sykes, 105 (San Francisco: Jossey-Bass, 1999).

8. Hess, "Dilemmas of Democracy Education"; Natasha Levinson, "Deliberative Democracy 101," in *Philosophy of Education 1998*, ed. Steven Tozer, 233 (Urbana, IL: Philosophy of Education Society, 1999).

9. Dan C. Lortie, *Schoolteacher: A Sociological Study* (Chicago: University of Chicago Press, 1975).

10. Lindsay Clare, Ronald Gallimore, and G. Genevieve Patthey-Chavez, "Using Moral Dilemmas in Children's Literature As a Vehicle for Moral Education and Teaching Reading Comprehension," *Journal of Moral Education* 25, no. 3 (1996): 325–41; Gretchen McAllister, "The Role of Empathy in Teaching Culturally Diverse Students: A Qualitative Study of Teachers' Beliefs," *Journal of Teacher Education* 53, no. 5 (2002): 434.

11. Alan J. Reiman and Sandra DeAngelis Peace, "Promoting Teachers' Moral Reasoning and Collaborative Inquiry Performance: A Developmental Role-Taking and Guided Inquiry Study," *Journal of Moral Education* 31, no. 1 (2002): 56; Hilda Borko, "Professional Development and Teacher Learning: Mapping the Terrain," *Educational Researcher* 33, no. 8 (2004): 3–15; Judith Warren Little, "Inside Teacher Community: Representations of Classroom Practice," *Teachers College Record* 105, no. 6 (2003): 913–45.

12. See, for example, Stefan Dasho and Sylvia Kendzior, "Toward a Caring Community of Learning for Teachers: Staff Development to Support the Child Development Project" (paper presented at the annual meeting of the American Educational Research Association, San Francisco, April 1995); Pritchard, *Reasonable Children*, 76.

13. Simon, *Moral Questions*, 207, 210, 218.

14. James A. Banks and Cherry A. McGee Banks, eds., *Multicultural Education: Issues and Perspectives*, 4th ed. (New York: Wiley, 2001); Simon, *Moral Questions*, 226, 246, 247.

15. Carolyn Gecan and Bernadette Mulholland-Glaze, "The Teacher's Place in the Formation of Students' Character," *Journal of Education* 175, no. 2 (1993): 45–57.

16. Peg Hill, "The 3Rs in the Inland Empire," *Social Studies Review, Religion, and the Public Schools* 40, no. 2 (2001): 39–46.

17. Marc W. Brown, "Christmas Trees, Carols, and Santa Claus: The Dichotomy of the First Amendment in the Public Schools and How the Implementation of a Religion Policy Affected a Community," *Journal of Law and Education* 28, no. 2 (1999): 145–92.

18. Coalition of Essential Schools University 2001 internal program evaluation, conducted in April 2002.

CHAPTER 8

1. David B. Wong, *Moral Relativity* (Berkeley: University of California Press, 1984), 8; Michael Walzer, "Education, Democratic Citizenship and Multiculturalism," in *Democratic Education in a Multicultural State*, ed. Yael Tamir, 30 (Oxford: Blackwell, 1995).

2. Theodore R. Sizer and Nancy Faust Sizer, "Grappling," *Phi Delta Kappan* 81, no. 3 (1999): 188.

3. See, for example, Berkowitz, "The Science of Character Education," in *Bringing in a New Era* and Constance A. Flanagan and Sukhdeep Gill, "Adolescents' Social Integration and Affection for the Polity: Processes for Different Racial/Ethnic Groups" (paper presented at the conference "Who Gets Involved?," sponsored by the Society for Research in Child Development, Albuquerque, NM, 1999). These researchers contend that public schools' insistence on a civic ethic holds increasing importance in our diverse society. They cite research underscoring the importance of relationships in schools, in particular how significant figures (e.g., teachers, administrators) treat others in students' presence. Teachers' behaviors and the tone and example they set for civility, tolerance, and fairness can significantly influence students' developing civic commitments.

4. See, for example, Alan L. Lockwood, "A Letter to Character Educators," *Educational Leadership* 51, no. 3 (1993): 72–75; Elizabeth Leistler Bruggeman and Kathleen J. Hart, "Cheating, Lying, and Moral Reasoning By Religious and Secular High School Students," *Journal of Educational Research* 89, no. 6 (1996): 340–44; Joseph Guttmann, "Cognitive Morality and Cheating Behavior in Religious and Secular School Children," *Journal of Educational Research* 77, no. 4 (1984): 249–54; Patrick Ferguson, "Impacts on Social and Political Participation," in *Handbook of Research on Social Studies Teaching and Learning*, ed. J. P. Shaver, 385–99 (New York: Macmillan, 1991), cited in Patricia G. Avery, "The Future of Political Participation in Civic Education," in *The Future of the Social Studies* (Boulder, CO: Social Science Education Consortium, 1994), 48.

5. Damon and Colby, "Education and Moral Commitment," 34.

6. Callan, "Autonomy, Child Rearing, and Good Lives," in *The Political and Moral Status of Children*, 139.

7. Purpel, *The Moral and Spiritual Crisis in Education*, 68.

Index